W9-DHW-929

GRADE
6

Social Studies

ISBN-13: 978-1-4190-3905-8
ISBN-10:   1-4190-3905-9

The paper used in this book comes from sustainable resources.

Printed in the United States of America.
1 2 3 4 5 6 7 8   862   14 13 12 11 10 09 08 07

Steck Vaughn™
A Harcourt Achieve Imprint

www.HarcourtSchoolSupply.com

Contents

Introduction

Social studies focuses on developing knowledge and skill in history, geography, culture, economics, civics, and government. It also focuses on people and their interaction with each other and the world in which they live. *Core Skills: Social Studies* addresses these areas of study and correlates with national social studies curriculum. With this book, students can:

- gain a better understanding of their country and its history

- practice map and geography skills

- work with charts and other graphic devices

The book features 20 chapter lessons on a variety of social studies topics. It also includes:

- interactive questions about the text or pictures

- chapter checkups

- unit skill builders to enhance social studies skills

- unit tests

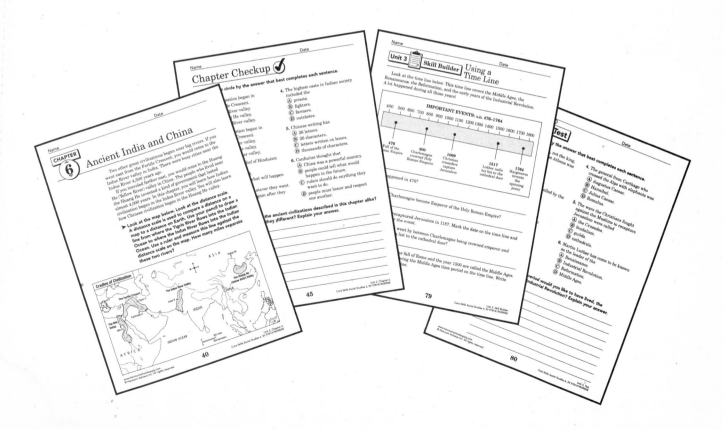

CHAPTER 1

A World of People

Think about the people you know. How are they different from one another? Is one person always laughing and joking? Is another shy and quiet? There are probably many differences you can think of among your friends, your family, and other people you know.

The people you know are just a few of the many people on Earth. In this chapter, you will learn how people are both different and the same all over the world.

The Home We All Share

Earth is home to many different people.

Today, Earth is the home of more than 6 billion people. Like the people you know, people around the world are different from one another in some ways. For example, they speak different languages.

➤ **Look at the pictures of people on this page. What differences can you see among some of Earth's people?**

_____

_____

People around the world are also the same in many ways. For example, all people need fresh water and certain kinds of food to stay healthy. They also need clothes to wear and places to live. Perhaps most important, people need other people. They need one another to learn and to teach, and to protect one another from danger.

To meet these many needs, people form groups called **communities**. A community can be as small as a tiny village or as large as a big city. You live in a community. By living and working together in communities, people can do things they could not do alone.

People and Places

People have formed communities in many different places on Earth. One reason people decide to live in a certain place is that the **natural environment** is good. The natural environment includes all the natural things that exist in a place. For example, mountains, deserts, seas, and rivers are part of what we call the natural environment. Weather, plants, and animals are also part of the natural environment.

Thousands of years ago, people formed communities near rivers so they could use the water to grow food. People also needed to be near rivers so they could get drinking water easily.

We have learned a lot about these early communities through the work of **archaeologists**. Archaeologists are people who study how humans lived long ago. Archaeologists study **artifacts**—objects used and left by people long ago.

➤ **List two other reasons people might want to live near a lake or a river.**

_____

_____

From space, Earth looks like a beautiful blue ball. When you look at Earth from space, you can see clouds, land, and water.

Core Skills Social Studies 6, SV 9781419039058

Different Ways of Life

The natural environment helps people decide how they will live in a place. For example, if the weather is usually cold, people will wear heavy clothes to keep warm. If they live near the ocean, they might learn how to use a boat. How does the natural environment of your community affect how you live?

➤ **Look at the picture below. List one way the natural environment affects how these people live.**

A community's way of life is called its **culture**. Culture includes how people dress and act. It also includes the foods they eat, the languages they speak, and the kinds of buildings they live and work in. Culture includes their religion and the holidays they celebrate.

One important part of a community's culture is its **economy**. The economy of a community is the way people make, buy, and sell things. How do the adults in your family earn their living? Their jobs are a part of your community's economy.

Another important part of a community's culture is its **government**. The government of a people is the way they choose their leaders and make their laws.

Changes in Today's World

The natural environment of a place can help people decide what to wear and what kinds of houses to build. But people can also change the natural environment. Whenever people cut down trees to build houses or plant crops, they change the natural environment.

Today, people can change the environment in ways that were not possible in the past. We can heat or cool huge spaces like football stadiums and shopping centers. We can make giant lakes in the middle of a desert. These things are possible because we have the **technology** to do them. Technology is the tools, materials, and knowledge people use to make things.

With the help of new technology, we can now build large communities in places where people could not live thousands of years ago. Food, water, and other goods that people need can be moved quickly to these communities from faraway places. This can happen because technology has made it possible to travel long distances in short periods of time.

➤ **Think of some important ways in which technology makes your life easier or more enjoyable.**

Hello Out There!

For much of human history, it was slow and dangerous to cross mountain ranges, deserts, or oceans. Until about 150 years ago, crops and other goods could be moved only as quickly as animals or boats could carry them. So most people usually spent their lives in one place.

Today, you can sit in an airplane and fly over mountains or oceans. You can pick up a telephone, or turn on a radio or television, and **communicate** with any place on Earth. When people communicate, they exchange information. Now your computer can allow you to exchange information with anyone anywhere about any subject.

➤ **Look at the chart on this page. What are the slowest and fastest ways to cross the United States?**

_____

_____

Traveling Time

How long would it take to cross the United States . . . ?

By wagon train	About 7 months
By train	About $3\frac{1}{2}$ days
By stagecoach	About 1 month
By jet airplane	About 5 hours
By auto, early 1900s	About 65 days
By auto today	About 6 days
On foot	About 6 months

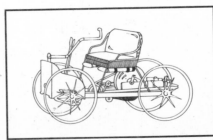

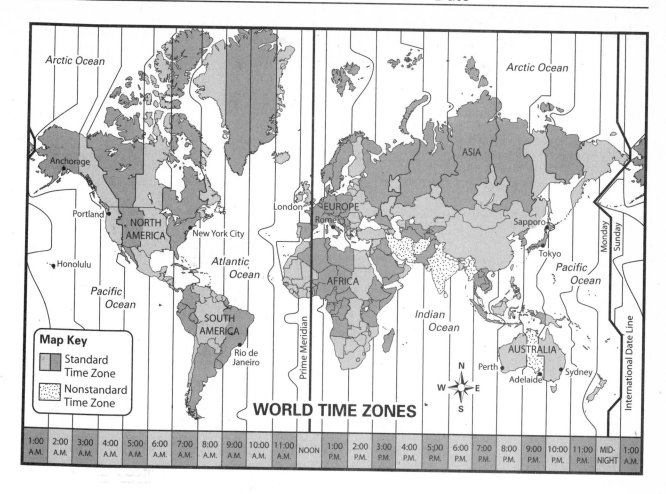

WORLD TIME ZONES

| 1:00 A.M. | 2:00 A.M. | 3:00 A.M. | 4:00 A.M. | 5:00 A.M. | 6:00 A.M. | 7:00 A.M. | 8:00 A.M. | 9:00 A.M. | 10:00 A.M. | 11:00 A.M. | NOON | 1:00 P.M. | 2:00 P.M. | 3:00 P.M. | 4:00 P.M. | 5:00 P.M. | 6:00 P.M. | 7:00 P.M. | 8:00 P.M. | 9:00 P.M. | 10:00 P.M. | 11:00 P.M. | MID-NIGHT | 1:00 A.M. |

Time Zones

At any single moment, it is not the same time of day in different places on Earth. This is because Earth rotates toward the east. As you travel west, the time is one hour earlier in each time zone. As you travel east, the time is one hour later. So different places on Earth have sunlight at different times. To keep track of these differences, the world is divided into 24 time zones, one for each hour of the day.

The speed of travel and communication today has made Earth seem smaller. People traveling by airplane can pass through several time zones in a short period of time.

Look at the map above. When it is 7 A.M. in New York City, it is 1 P.M. in Rome. When it is 7 A.M. in New York, it is 9 P.M. *the next day* in Tokyo.

► **Draw a line between Portland and Rio de Janeiro. What time is it in Rio when it is 4 A.M. in Portland?**

_____

Chapter Checkup ✓

➤ **Darken the circle by the answer that best completes each sentence.**

1. People around the world are the same because
   - (A) they all speak the same language.
   - (B) they all wear the same clothes.
   - (C) they all need fresh water and food.
   - (D) they all live near water.

2. A community is
   - (A) a group of people living and working together.
   - (B) a body of water.
   - (C) a type of home that can be moved easily.
   - (D) a kind of transportation.

3. Mountains, weather, plants, and animals are all part of
   - (A) the culture of a community.
   - (B) the natural environment.
   - (C) the economy of a community.
   - (D) new technology.

4. *Culture* means
   - (A) the natural environment of a place.
   - (B) buildings.
   - (C) a community's way of life.
   - (D) language.

5. The way people make, buy, and sell things is
   - (A) the economy.
   - (B) the culture.
   - (C) transportation.
   - (D) the environment.

6. The world is divided into time zones because
   - (A) travel by airplane can surprise you.
   - (B) the speed of travel today has made Earth seem smaller.
   - (C) people are now able to visit one another easily.
   - (D) different places on Earth have sunlight at different times.

Thinking & Writing

Why do people often change the natural environment that surrounds them?

_____

_____

_____

_____

_____

 CHAPTER 2 Geography of Earth

Have you ever flown in a plane? If you have, you might already know something about Earth's **geography**. What did you see when you looked out the window? Mountains? The waves of an ocean?

You might have seen both mountains and the ocean, because Earth's surface changes from place to place. Geography is the science that describes Earth's surface. It tries to explain how and why Earth changes. It also explains how people affect Earth and how Earth affects people.

Earth's Land Regions

There are four main types of land regions found on Earth. They are **mountains, highlands, plateaus,** and **plains**.

➤ **Look at the picture below. What kind of land region is shown in this picture?**

Mountain and highland regions are areas of land that rise far above sea level. These regions include many mountains, high hills, and deep valleys. About one fifth of Earth's land surface is mountainous.

There are two great mountain regions on Earth. One can be found along the western side of North and South America. In the western part of North America, the region includes the Sierra Nevada, the Cascade Mountains, and the Rocky Mountains. In South America, the region is made up of the Andes Mountains.

The other mountain region goes through Europe and Asia. It includes the Himalayas and the Alps. The Himalaya Mountains are the highest mountains in the world. The highest peak is Mount Everest. It is nearly 30,000 feet above sea level. Mount Everest is the highest mountain on Earth.

➤ **Look at the two photos at the bottom of this page. Which two of the four main types of land regions do they show?**

Plains and Plateaus

Plains are flat lands that are very close to sea level. Most people on Earth live in plains regions. It is easier to farm and build houses on land that is flat.

Plateaus are high lands that are usually flat. A plateau often rises up sharply on at least one side. Some plateaus rise up from the ground on all four sides.

➤ **Look at the map below. Put an X near the Patagonian Plateau and the Great Central Plain. Near what mountain range is each of these plateaus located?**

_____

➤ **Find the region on the map where you live. Write the name of the land region closest to your community.**

_____

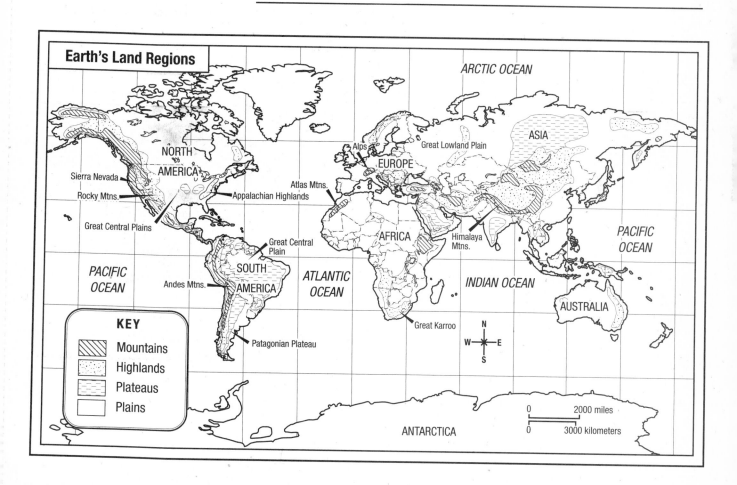

Earth's Climate Regions

Not all plains and plateaus are the same. Earth's land regions are different because of their **climate**. The climate is how hot, cold, wet, or dry a place is year after year.

➤ **Look at the map key below. What are the six different kinds of climate found on Earth?**

_____

In most tropical climates, heavy rains fall all year long. The rain and hot climate produce thick **rain forests**. Because there is so much rainfall, trees and other plants grow very quickly.

Earth's Climate Regions

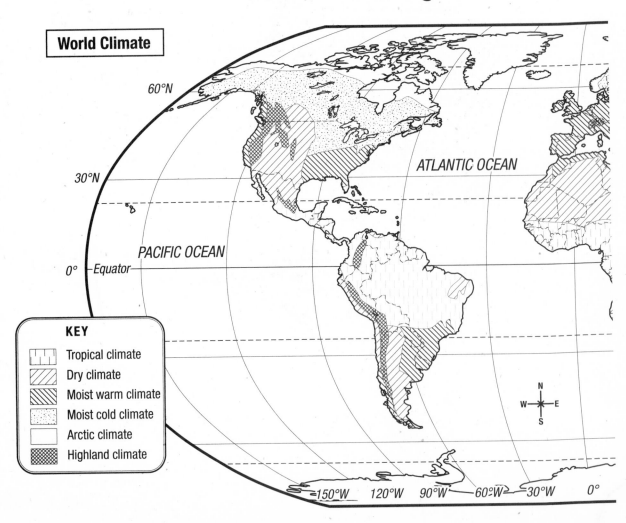

World Climate

KEY
Tropical climate
Dry climate
Moist warm climate
Moist cold climate
Arctic climate
Highland climate

Unit 1, Chapter 2
Core Skills Social Studies 6, SV 9781419039058

Some land regions on Earth get very little rain. They are called **deserts**. A desert can be a hot, dry place where few plants can grow.

Arctic regions are very cold. They are located north of the Arctic Circle and south of the Antarctic Circle. These regions have huge sheets of ice called **glaciers**. These cold regions also get very little rainfall. They are deserts, too.

Moist warm and moist cold climates both receive about 20 to 40 inches of rain a year. Winters are longer and colder in moist cold climates.

➤ **Look at the part of the map below. Find the Tropic of Cancer. Are moist warm and moist cold climates found mostly above or below this line on the map?**

_____

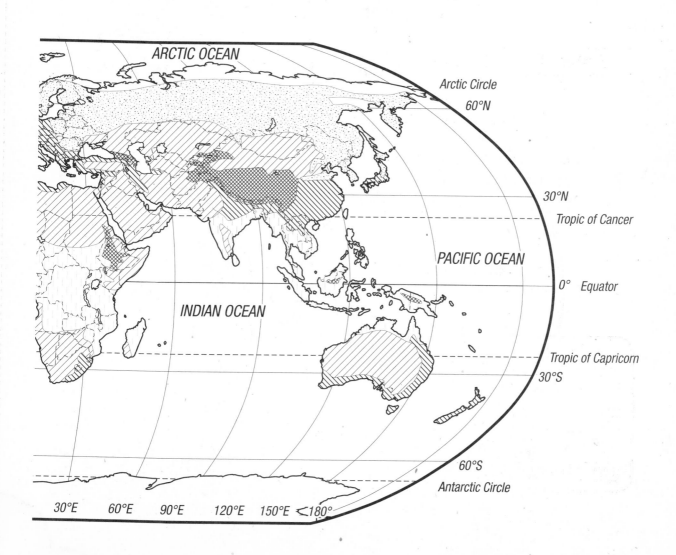

How Climate Affects Earth

Have you wondered why there are mountains in some places on Earth and plains in others? Earth's climate has shaped much of its geography.

Several times in the distant past, Earth's climate became much cooler. Huge glaciers spread over many areas of Earth. These sheets of ice cut into Earth, creating valleys and plains. When the glaciers melted during warmer periods, some of them created rivers and lakes.

➤ **Where are glaciers found today?**

_____

Strong winds can also change the surface of Earth, picking up soil in one place and dropping it in another. This is called **erosion**.

Many forces have changed the surface of Earth in the past and still do so today.

World Population

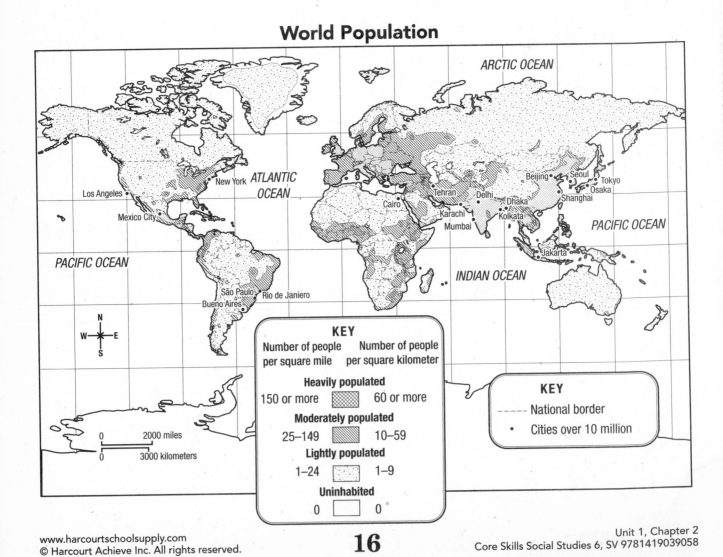

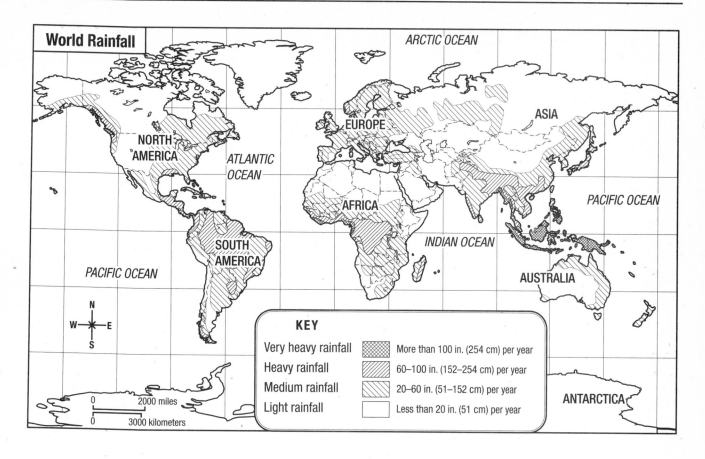

Where Do People Live?

The map on page 16 is a population map. It shows where people live on Earth.

The map on this page shows how much rain or snow falls in a year in different regions on Earth. We call this a rainfall map because most **precipitation**, or moisture, falls as rain.

Look at the map above and study the map key.

➤ **Pick two areas on the map that receive light rainfall. Now find these areas on the population map on page 16. These areas are probably lightly populated. Find an area on the rainfall map that receives medium rainfall. This area is probably heavily or moderately populated.**

What connection can you make between world rainfall and world population?

_____

As you can see, climate helps people decide where to make their homes.

Chapter Checkup ✓

▶ **Darken the circle by the answer that best completes each sentence.**

1. Four main land regions on Earth are called
   - (A) plains, valleys, mountains, and highlands.
   - (B) canyons, plateaus, mountains, and highlands.
   - (C) mountains, highlands, plateaus, and plains.
   - (D) oceans, mountains, highlands, and plains.

2. The highest mountains in the world are the
   - (A) Andes.
   - (B) Himalayas.
   - (C) Great Central Plains.
   - (D) deserts.

3. The six main climate regions on Earth are called tropical, dry, moist warm, moist cold, highland, and
   - (A) arctic.
   - (B) glacier.
   - (C) hot.
   - (D) wet.

4. Land regions on Earth that get very little rain are called
   - (A) deserts.
   - (B) valleys.
   - (C) rain forests.
   - (D) erosions.

5. Earth's climate has shaped much of its geography through
   - (A) erosion and population.
   - (B) glaciers and rain forests.
   - (C) the Tropic of Cancer and the equator.
   - (D) erosion and glaciers.

6. Population numbers and rainfall are connected because
   - (A) few people live in areas that have medium rainfall.
   - (B) most people live in areas that have no rainfall.
   - (C) most people live in areas that have medium or heavy rainfall.
   - (D) there are glaciers in areas of light rainfall.

Thinking & Writing

Why do most people live in plains regions?

_____

_____

_____

_____

_____

18
Unit 1, Chapter 2
Core Skills Social Studies 6, SV 9781419039058

CHAPTER 3

Earth's Resources

Imagine that you are planning to take a long trip through outer space. What will you need to take with you? Remember, you must take everything that you will need to live. You will need food, water, air, clothing, tools, and **fuel**. Oil and coal are examples of fuels that are used to run engines. All of these things are **resources**. Resources are the things people use to meet their needs.

You use resources every day. Every time you eat food or drink water, you are using resources. Earth is like a giant spaceship that contains the resources humans need to survive.

➤ **Oil is a natural resource found deep in the ground. How does it help us travel long distances?**

_____

_____

Renewable and Nonrenewable Resources

The resources that people use on Earth can be divided into two different groups: renewable and nonrenewable. Nature provides people with **renewable resources**. Air, water, and all living things, including animals and plants, are renewable resources. There will always be more of these resources, as long as people use them carefully.

Wind turbines use air to generate electricity.

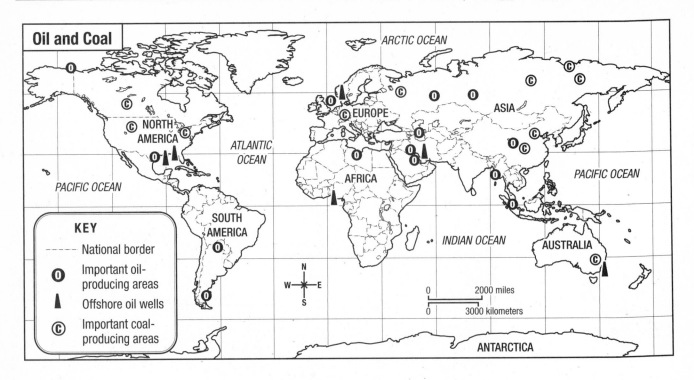

Nonrenewable resources are those resources that Earth made long ago. They cannot be made again, except over a very long period of time. These resources were once the remains of plant and animal life. Over a period of millions of years, heat and pressure deep inside Earth turned these remains into such things as oil, coal, and natural gas. Many of these nonrenewable resources are important because they can be used as fuel.

▶ **Look at the map on this page. Circle the offshore oil wells on the map. Name two continents that have offshore oil wells.**

_____

Coal, Oil, and Natural Gas

Today, the world's main sources of energy are coal, oil, and natural gas. Beginning in the 1800s, coal was burned to make steam. The steam was used to run engines in trains, ships, and other machines. Coal is still used today. It supplies about 30 percent of the world's energy.

Oil is used to make gasoline. It is also used for airplane fuel and to heat homes. Natural gas is used to heat homes and factories.

Farm Products and Lumber

Plants and trees are another resource that people use. Farm products such as wheat, vegetables, and fruits are important because all people depend on them for food.

Trees also provide us with an important resource—lumber. With lumber from forests, we build houses and make paper.

➤ **Complete the following sentence. Lumber is an example of a renewable resource because**

_____

_____

Conservation

What do you think will happen as people continue to use nonrenewable resources? Many of these resources could run out very soon. This is one reason why people today are thinking about **conservation**. *Conservation* means "saving." We must save resources and use them carefully.

It is not just nonrenewable resources that need to be saved. Air, soil, and water are renewable resources. They can be replaced, but if they are not used wisely, they can become dirty and unusable. For this reason, it is important to save both nonrenewable and renewable resources.

Saving a Rain Forest

Saving natural regions on Earth is also a part of conservation. Many people now believe that rain forests found in tropical climates are an important resource for all life on Earth.

The largest rain forest in the world is the Amazon rain forest in South America. This forest has billions of trees and other plants. Plants make oxygen. Some scientists believe that the Amazon forest makes up to 60 percent of the world's oxygen.

Yet in recent years, people moving into the Amazon have cut and burned down millions of trees. If this continues, the Amazon rain forest may be destroyed. Many scientists believe that all life on Earth would be hurt by the loss of the Amazon rain forest. For this reason, people all over the world are working to save the Amazon rain forest.

➤ **Describe one way people are working on the conservation of natural resources.**

_____

_____

Pollution

Factories, automobiles, and machines all help make our lives easier. However, they also create many problems. **Pollution**, or the dirtying of Earth's air and water, is one of them.

Pollution is not a new problem for people. Since the beginning of human life, people have created garbage. They have used resources and thrown things away. However, in the past, there were fewer people on Earth than there are today. Fewer people used fewer resources. They also created less pollution.

Large sections of the Amazon rain forest have been burned or cut down in recent years.

Air Pollution

The air around us sometimes contains many kinds of pollution. Coal and oil that are burned to make electricity release gases into the air. So does the gasoline used in automobiles. Polluted air can make it hard to breathe. It can also harm crops and animals.

➤ **Do you think trying to conserve resources like coal and oil would help make the air less polluted? Explain your answer.**

_____

_____

Water Pollution

Water pollution happens when garbage and other wastes are put into rivers and oceans. In the past, factories emptied polluted water into these bodies of water. Later, plants were built to clean the water. The plants helped, but water pollution still exists today.

Oil spills are a dangerous kind of pollution. These happen when large ships that carry oil spill the oil into oceans or harbors. Accidents sometimes make holes in the sides of the ships. Then oil spills into the water.

A large oil spill happened in Alaska in 1989. Thousands of gallons of thick black oil spread over the water and onto the shore. The oil killed many kinds of animals, including seabirds, eagles, otters, seals, and bears.

Nobody likes oil spills. People do not want to ruin Earth. People today are working hard to find answers to the pollution problem. Perhaps in the years ahead we can find more ways to save our resources.

Water pollution can be a serious problem in places that have factories.

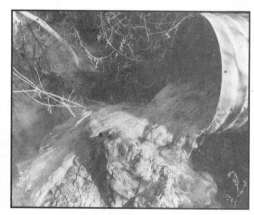

Chapter Checkup ✓

➤ **Darken the circle by the answer that best completes each sentence.**

1. Water, air, and plants are examples of
   - Ⓐ the world's main sources of energy.
   - Ⓑ renewable resources.
   - Ⓒ pollution.
   - Ⓓ nonrenewable resources.

2. Oil, coal, and minerals are examples of
   - Ⓐ nonrenewable resources.
   - Ⓑ rain forest resources.
   - Ⓒ renewable resources.
   - Ⓓ food resources.

3. The world's main energy resources are oil, coal, and
   - Ⓐ lumber.
   - Ⓑ water.
   - Ⓒ natural gas.
   - Ⓓ electricity.

4. People who are concerned about conservation want to
   - Ⓐ create more nonrenewable resources.
   - Ⓑ use resources wisely.
   - Ⓒ use up nonrenewable resources.
   - Ⓓ destroy natural resources.

5. Pollution is caused by
   - Ⓐ factories and machines that make the air and water dirty.
   - Ⓑ conservation of natural resources.
   - Ⓒ creation of renewable resources.
   - Ⓓ cleaning natural resources.

6. The largest rain forest in the world is in
   - Ⓐ North America.
   - Ⓑ Europe.
   - Ⓒ Alaska.
   - Ⓓ South America.

Thinking & Writing

Why do you think more and more people think conservation is important today?

_____

_____

_____

_____

_____

_____

Unit 1 | **Skill Builder** | # Reading a Time Zone Map

As you know, Earth has 24 time zones. But did you know that if you went from New York City to Honolulu, Hawaii, you would cross six time zones? Look at the map below.

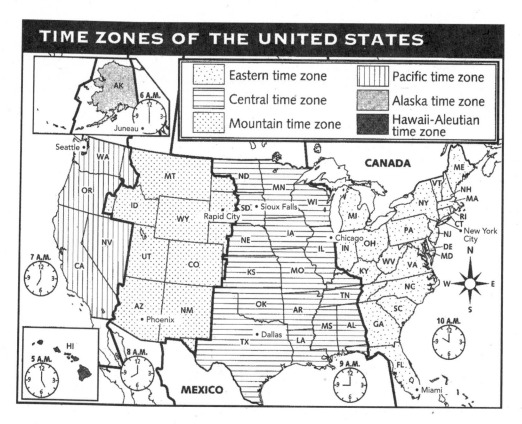

TIME ZONES OF THE UNITED STATES

1. At 9:00 P.M. in Seattle, Washington, what time is it in Juneau, Alaska?

_____

2. How many time zones does Florida have?

_____

3. If it is 7:30 A.M. in Dallas, Texas, what time is it in Chicago, Illinois?

_____

4. Suppose you left Sioux Falls, South Dakota, and headed west. How would you reset your watch when you reached Rapid City, South Dakota?

_____

Unit 1  Test

➤ **Darken the circle by the answer that best completes each sentence.**

1. The tools, materials, and knowledge people use to make things are called
   - Ⓐ environment.
   - Ⓑ technology.
   - Ⓒ economy.
   - Ⓓ time zones.

2. The way people make, buy, and sell things is called the
   - Ⓐ environment.
   - Ⓑ government.
   - Ⓒ economy.
   - Ⓓ community.

3. The four main land regions on Earth are mountains, highlands, plateaus, and
   - Ⓐ plains.
   - Ⓑ volcanoes.
   - Ⓒ forests.
   - Ⓓ grasslands.

4. Regions of Earth with tropical climates are
   - Ⓐ hot and dry.
   - Ⓑ hot and wet.
   - Ⓒ mild and dry.
   - Ⓓ cool and wet.

5. Strong winds picking up the soil in one place and dropping it in another is
   - Ⓐ deserts.
   - Ⓑ glaciers.
   - Ⓒ erosion.
   - Ⓓ geography.

6. Resources that Earth made long ago that cannot be made again are
   - Ⓐ renewable.
   - Ⓑ nonrenewable.
   - Ⓒ food plants.
   - Ⓓ rain forests.

Describe the place you live in terms of its geography, climate, time zone, and resources. Then describe one other place in the world you would most like to live.

_____

_____

_____

_____

_____

_____

_____

CHAPTER

4 The Fertile Crescent

Have you ever stood at the top of a tall building in a large city? What did you see below you? You probably saw crowded streets and people rushing into stores and offices. Maybe you saw a busy highway filled with cars and trucks. All these things are a part of modern **civilization**.

What is civilization? The word comes from an old word that means "someone who lives in a city." Yet civilization means more than just living in cities. In this chapter, you will learn how one of the world's first civilizations began.

➤ **Look at the picture below. In what ways are modern cities different from this picture of one of the first cities?**

_____

_____

Mesopotamia

One of the first civilizations was in Mesopotamia. Today this region is part of a country called Iraq. Two rivers ran through Mesopotamia, the Tigris and the Euphrates.

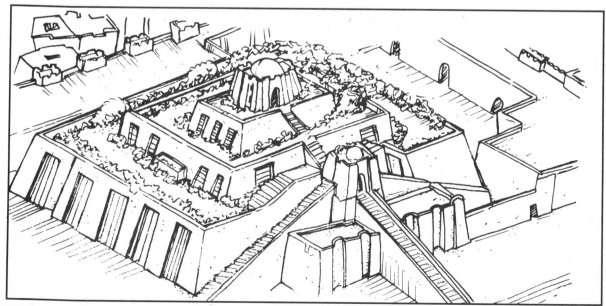

In Mesopotamia, the place of worship was the center of the community.

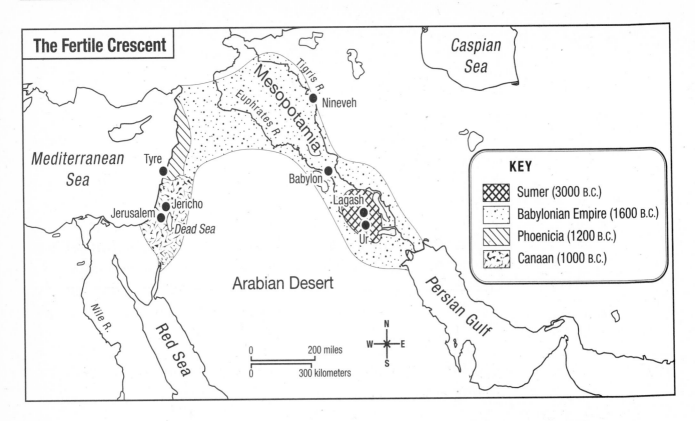

The Fertile Crescent

The land between the Tigris and Euphrates Rivers was good for farming. The rivers provided water for crops. Land that is good for farming is called **fertile**. For this reason, the land of Mesopotamia is called the Fertile Crescent.

➤ **Look at the map on this page. Write the names of the four cities that were near the Tigris and Euphrates Rivers in Mesopotamia.**

_____

_____

What Makes a Civilization?

We study the ancient civilization of Mesopotamia because it influenced later civilizations, including our own. But civilization did not happen overnight. Let's look at the five steps that people took to develop civilization over 5,000 years ago.

First, people learned how to grow crops. They also discovered how to **domesticate**, or tame and use, animals. This was an important step. Before people knew how to farm, they had to hunt animals and find wild plants for food.

Second, people began to build permanent homes. Before civilization, humans moved from place to place. They lived in caves or tents.

People moved from place to place because they had to follow the animals they hunted for food. But with crops and domesticated animals, people could live in one place and build houses. Once this happened, towns, and then cities, began to grow.

Third, people began to develop technology. You remember that technology is the use of tools to help people in their work. Early people learned to make weapons from metal instead of stone. They also invented such important tools as the wheel.

Fourth, people made intellectual achievements. *Intellectual* means "having to do with the mind." These achievements included the invention of writing and the calendar. People could now write stories and keep records of their crops. Calendars helped people keep track of time.

Finally, people began to create laws and rules to help them live together. In a city, laws are needed to keep order among the different people who live there.

Civilization in Sumer

Sumer became the first large area of farming villages in Mesopotamia. Find Sumer on the map on page 28. The people of Sumer, called the Sumerians, created the first civilization in Mesopotamia about 5,000 years ago.

One of the most important steps made by this civilization was the invention of a written language. Writing was invented probably to meet people's needs for keeping records and lists. Soon the Sumerians came up with a way to keep track of what they bought and sold. Little by little, a complete system of writing was invented in Sumer. It was called **cuneiform**.

➤ **The Sumerians first used writing to keep records and lists. What else can people do with writing? Create your own writing system. Show some characters below.**

_____

_____

_____

_____

The civilization of Sumer reached its high point about 4,000 years ago. The Sumerians had learned how to **irrigate** their crops. This means they built ditches and canals to bring water from the rivers to dry land. They lived in large walled cities. At the center of each city was a **temple** called a **ziggurat**. A temple is a building where people pray to a god or gods. Here the Sumerians prayed to their gods and goddesses for good crops.

Soon ideas from Sumer began spreading. Traders came and went from the cities of Sumer. When they traveled, these traders took with them the knowledge of Sumer's inventions.

The Babylonians

About 3,000 years ago, new groups of people began moving into Mesopotamia. One of the largest and most powerful of these groups was the Babylonians. These people were named for Babylon, the city they built in Mesopotamia.

▶ **Look at the map on page 28. Which direction is Babylon from the city of Ur in Sumer?**

_____

Under a king named Hammurabi, the Babylonians **conquered**, or defeated, the Sumerians. They ruled all of Mesopotamia. But the Babylonians learned a lot from the Sumerians. The Babylonians built large farms and ziggurats and wrote in cuneiform.

Hammurabi's Laws

Hammurabi was not only a powerful warrior. He also developed a set of laws to help rule his kingdom. Hammurabi collected laws from all over Mesopotamia. He chose the ones he thought were fair. These laws had to do with land, money, business, and family life. The main idea behind Hammurabi's laws was that strong people should not hurt weak people.

Hammurabi, king of Babylon, is shown standing before a Sumerian god.

The Hebrews

The Hebrews were another group of people who originally lived in Mesopotamia. A great Hebrew leader named Abraham led the Hebrews from Sumer into the land of Canaan. This land now lies in Israel and Lebanon.

The Hebrews lived in Canaan for many years. Then a **drought**, a long period of time without rain, began to kill their crops. The Hebrews then went to Egypt, a country you will read about in the next chapter. The Hebrews were turned into **slaves** by the Egyptians. A slave is someone who is owned by another person. In time, a great Hebrew leader named Moses led the Hebrews back to Canaan.

➤ **What caused the Hebrews to leave Canaan?**

_____

_____

The Ten Commandments

In Mesopotamia and Egypt, most people believed in many gods. The Hebrews, however, believed in only one god. The belief in one god is called **monotheism**. Today we call the religion of the ancient Hebrews **Judaism**. People who follow Judaism are called Jews.

According to the holy writing of Judaism, it was God who told Moses to lead the Hebrews out of Egypt and across the desert to Canaan. This journey was called the **Exodus**, which means "departure."

The Hebrews followed laws during the Exodus. The most important of these laws were the Ten Commandments. Several religions believe that God gave the Ten Commandments to Moses while the Hebrews were in the desert.

The Ten Commandments became the most important of all Hebrew laws. They taught people to honor their parents and to love one another. They do not allow people to lie, steal, cheat, or kill.

➤ **In what ways are the Ten Commandments similar to many laws that we have today?**

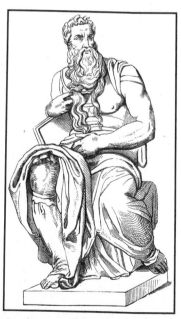

Sculpture of Moses by Michelangelo

_____

_____

Name _____   Date _____

Chapter Checkup ✓

➤ **Darken the circle by the answer that best completes each sentence.**

1. The ancient land of Mesopotamia is also called
   Ⓐ Babylon.
   Ⓑ Sumer.
   Ⓒ the Fertile Crescent.
   Ⓓ the Exodus.

2. As one of the five steps to developing a civilization, people learned how to
   Ⓐ study other civilizations.
   Ⓑ grow crops and tame animals.
   Ⓒ find wild plants for food.
   Ⓓ hunt animals.

3. The form of writing that the Sumerian people developed was known as
   Ⓐ ziggurats.
   Ⓑ irrigation.
   Ⓒ temples.
   Ⓓ cuneiform.

4. Hammurabi's laws
   Ⓐ helped the Babylonians live together peacefully.
   Ⓑ were written for the Egyptians.
   Ⓒ were used to tame animals.
   Ⓓ were given to Moses for the Hebrews.

5. The Exodus was
   Ⓐ the trip the Hebrews made from Egypt to Canaan.
   Ⓑ the time when Hebrews were slaves in Egypt.
   Ⓒ the set of laws Moses gave the Hebrews.
   Ⓓ a city near the Euphrates River.

6. The Ten Commandments were
   Ⓐ laws Hammurabi gave the Babylonians.
   Ⓑ one of the steps people took to develop civilization.
   Ⓒ a Sumerian invention.
   Ⓓ laws the Hebrews followed.

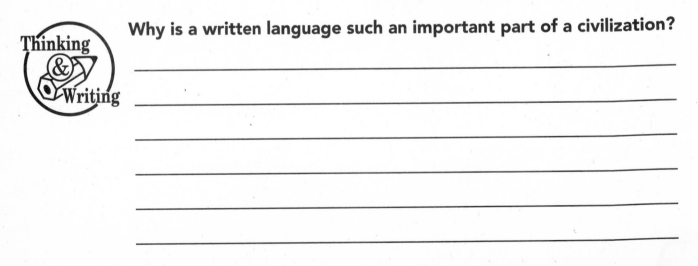

Thinking & Writing

Why is a written language such an important part of a civilization?

_____
_____
_____
_____
_____
_____

CHAPTER 5

Ancient Egypt

The Nile River is the longest river in the world. It is more than 4,000 miles long. It flows from a lake deep in Africa to the hot desert land of Egypt.

The people of Egypt need water from the Nile. Their country gets little rain. Thousands of years ago, one of the world's first civilizations began on the shores of this river.

The Nile River Valley

People began moving into the Nile River valley in Egypt over 10,000 years ago. They stayed because the land near the river was fertile.

➤ **How did rivers help the Sumerians and the Egyptians?**

_____

_____

The Sphinx has gazed across Egypt for centuries.

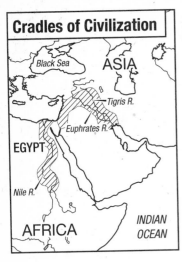

Cradles of Civilization

Every summer the Nile flooded the land around it. These floods left a layer of fertile soil on the land. Farmers planted their crops in the soil.

The Egyptians found that they could trap the floodwater from the river and save it. Farmers worked together to bring the floodwater to their farms. Soon people began to live and work together in small villages.

➤ **Look at the map on this page. Why was the Nile so important to Egypt?**

_____

_____

The First Pharaoh

Over time, the small villages became larger. About 5,000 years ago, a man named Menes ruled over several villages in Egypt. He soon brought all the villages in Egypt together under his leadership.

Menes became the first king of Egypt. Then he built a new capital city called Memphis. Menes also built a large palace for himself. After that, Egypt's king was always called the **pharaoh**, which meant "great palace" or "great house."

Government Under the Pharaoh

The pharaoh made laws for all the people of Egypt. Everyone in Egypt worked for the pharaoh in some way. For example, the farmers in Egypt had to give some of the food that they grew to the pharaoh.

The second most powerful group of people were the nobles, who ran the government. Artists—makers of statues and buildings—had less power than the nobles. Farmers and other workers had little say in the government.

Both men and women had many of the same rights in Egypt. They could own a home, go to school, and buy and sell goods. Women in most other early civilizations did not have these rights.

Name _____   Date _____

Egyptian Religion

Like the people of Mesopotamia, the Egyptians believed in many gods. They believed that the sun was a god named Ra. Each day they watched as the sun rose. Then they watched as the sun traveled across the sky and set. In the morning, the Egyptians watched as the sun rose again.

The Egyptians thought that human life was like the sun. A person was born, just as the sun rose. A person died, just as the sun set. And just as the sun rose again after it set, the Egyptians believed a person would live again after death.

Certain things had to be done, however, to make sure this would happen. First, the bodies of dead people had to be protected. The Egyptians developed a way to protect bodies called **mummification**. They put chemicals on the bodies. Then they wrapped the bodies in long strips of cloth. Finally, they covered the wrapped bodies with a mixture like tar. This made them waterproof. Today, we call these preserved bodies mummies.

Second, the dead person had to be placed in a **tomb**. A tomb is a place or a building where the dead are buried. All the things the person might want in the next life were placed near the mummy. Food and water were put in the tomb for the dead person. Games, clothing, and other objects the person might need were also put in the tomb.

Wall paintings have been found in some tombs. They show the dead person doing things that he or she enjoyed in life. Some pictures show people fishing and swimming in the Nile. Others show people enjoying food with their friends. We have learned many things about ancient Egyptian life from these paintings.

➤ **Why might the Egyptians have wanted to paint pictures from their life on the walls of their tombs?**

_____

_____

_____

An Egyptian mummy

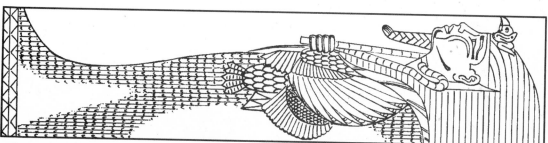

The Pyramids

The largest tombs were built for the pharaohs. Some pharaohs built tombs called **pyramids**. The largest pyramid in Egypt is called the Great Pyramid. It was built about 4,500 years ago. It is shaped like a triangle and is as tall as a 45-story building! About 100,000 people worked 20 years to build it. They used about two million blocks of stone in the Great Pyramid. Each stone weighed $2\frac{1}{2}$ tons.

How did the Egyptians build such big buildings without trucks and cranes? They probably used three simple machines: the lever, the ramp, and the wedge. The outer surface of the pyramid was covered with pure white limestone. This limestone came from quarries across the Nile in eastern Egypt. Scientists think that each stone was pushed up a ramp. Once the stones were in position, the ramp was built higher.

➤ **Many people helped build a pyramid. Look at the picture on this page. How did the Egyptians move the heavy stones?**

_____

_____

Building a pyramid was hard work.

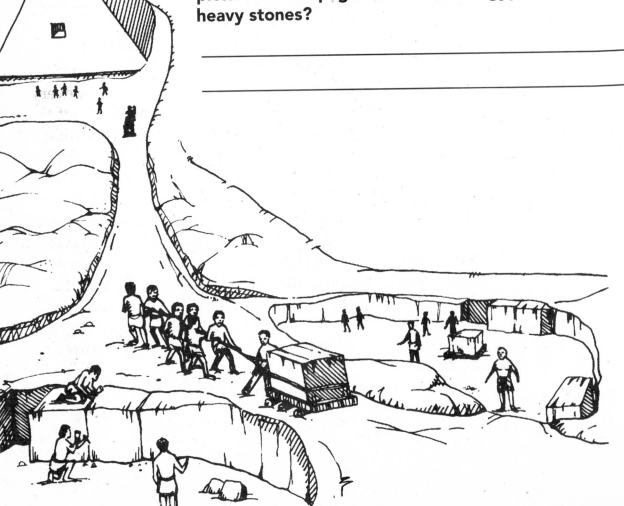

The golden mummy mask of King Tutankhamen

The Treasure of Tutankhamen

The tombs of the pharaohs were filled with many treasures. Over the centuries, however, most tombs were robbed or destroyed. One tomb, however, was not robbed. This was the tomb of a pharaoh named Tutankhamen. He was known as the boy-king because he died when he was only 18 years old.

Tutankhamen's tomb was discovered in 1922. The king's mummy lay inside a case made of solid gold. A gold mask covered the king's head. The tomb was filled with jewelry, furniture, clothes, weapons, and games. Tutankhamen's tomb helped people learn a lot about how people in ancient Egypt lived.

▶ **Look at the photograph on this page. How does it show that the pharaoh was important?**

_____

_____

Egyptian Contributions to Civilization

Like the Sumerians, the ancient Egyptians invented a calendar. They noticed that the Nile flood came once every 365 days. They also saw that the flood arrived at about the same time every year. This gave them the idea that time could be divided into equal periods. From this idea, the Egyptians made a calendar with days, months, and years.

The Egyptians also made a writing material called **papyrus**. They made papyrus from plants that grew along the Nile. They glued the stems together and then soaked and dried them. Our word *paper* comes from the word *papyrus*.

The Egyptians invented a kind of writing, just as the Sumerians did. The Egyptian writing system is called **hieroglyphics**, or picture writing. This is because Egyptian writing is made up of a series of pictures. Each picture stands for an object, an idea, an action, or a sound. When the pictures are put together, they form a language.

These hieroglyphics made up a written language that told a story.

You may wonder how people today are able to read hieroglyphics. About 200 years ago, a stone was found half buried in the Egyptian desert. Hieroglyphics were on the stone, as well as other languages, including Greek. Scientists were able to use these languages to figure out what the hieroglyphics meant.

➤ **Look at the picture on this page. What can you recognize from Egyptian picture writing?**

_____

_____

The Fall of Egypt

For more than a thousand years, Egypt was a proud and powerful country. The Egyptian people thought that their country would remain powerful forever. However, that did not happen.

About 3,000 years ago, Egypt began to grow weak. The pharaohs did not rule the people well. Then a number of floods did not bring enough water for farmers to grow crops.

Foreign armies soon began to invade Egypt. In the centuries that followed, Egypt was conquered by people from Mesopotamia. Later, it was conquered by the Greeks and then by the Romans. You will read about the civilizations of ancient Greece and Rome later in this book.

Ancient Egypt has left the world many treasures. Today, you can visit Egypt and explore the pyramid of a great pharaoh. You can go to a museum and see furniture, clothes, and games that once belonged to the boy-king Tutankhamen.

The ancient Egyptians were more than just great builders. Farmers, artists, government leaders, and builders all worked together to make one of the world's first great civilizations.

Name _____   Date _____

Chapter Checkup ✓

➤ **Darken the circle by the answer that best completes each sentence.**

1. The Nile River valley was similar to the lands of the Fertile Crescent because
   (A) there were no people or buildings there.
   (B) the land was not good for farming.
   (C) the land was fertile.
   (D) Egyptians lived in both places.

2. The pharaoh made
   (A) laws for all the people in Egypt.
   (B) canals to help farmers trap water.
   (C) papyrus for people to write on.
   (D) calendars to tell when the Nile would flood.

3. Egyptians believed that after death people
   (A) became gods and goddesses.
   (B) went to a foreign country.
   (C) changed into animals.
   (D) would live again.

4. The pyramids were
   (A) tombs for the Egyptian pharaohs.
   (B) tombs for Egyptian workers.
   (C) writing material the Egyptians used.
   (D) large Egyptian trading ships.

5. Egyptian contributions to civilization included
   (A) ships and metal tools.
   (B) new technology for farming.
   (C) a kind of paper, a written language, and a calendar.
   (D) a new way to catch fish.

6. The Egyptian system of writing is called
   (A) papyrus.
   (B) hieroglyphics.
   (C) pharaohs.
   (D) Tutankhamen.

Why do you think it is important to study ancient civilizations such as Egypt?

_____
_____
_____
_____
_____
_____

CHAPTER 6 Ancient India and China

Two other great civilizations began near big rivers. If you went east from the Fertile Crescent, you would come to the Indus River valley in India. There were busy cities near the Indus River 4,500 years ago.

If you traveled farther east, you would come to the Huang He (Yellow River) valley in China. The people who lived near the Huang He invented a kind of government that lasted almost 4,000 years. In this chapter, you will learn how Indian civilization began in the Indus River valley. You will also learn how Chinese civilization began in the Huang He valley.

➤ **Look at the map below. Look at the _distance scale_. A distance scale is used to compare a distance on a map to a distance on Earth. Use your pencil to draw a line from where the Tigris River flows into the Indian Ocean to where the Indus River flows into the Indian Ocean. Use a ruler and measure this line against the distance scale on the map. How many miles separate these two rivers?**

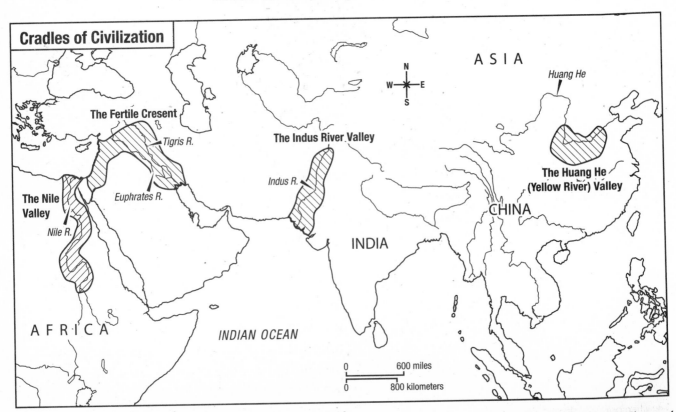

Mohenjo-Daro

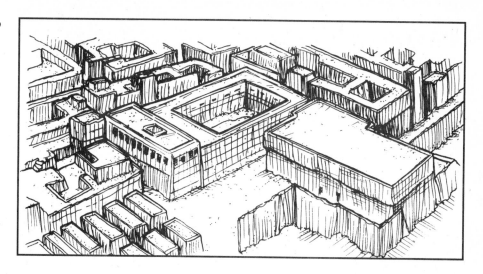

A Lost City

For a long time, no one even knew that there had once been ancient cities in the Indus River valley. Then, in the 1920s, archaeologists made an important discovery. They found cups and vases, coins, and jewelry buried in the soil. Beneath hills of earth, they found streets and houses. And they found the skeletons of people! The archaeologists realized they had found what was left of a ruined city. They named it Mohenjo-Daro, meaning the "city (or mound) of the dead."

Houses in Mohenjo-Daro were made of fine brick. More than 40,000 people once lived there. Like the Sumerians, the people of Mohenjo-Daro had a written language. They also had learned how to irrigate their crops.

The archaeologists discovered many things in Mohenjo-Daro that came from the Fertile Crescent. This showed that the people of Mohenjo-Daro and the Fertile Crescent had traded with one another.

A New People

A new group of people arrived in the Indus River valley over 3,000 years ago. They were a warlike people called Aryans. They conquered all the land around the Indus River. The culture of the Aryans changed life in India forever.

The Aryans brought with them a language called Sanskrit. Many languages that are spoken in India today developed from Sanskrit.

The Aryans also invented the **caste** system. The caste system divided people into groups. People who did the same type of work all belonged to the same caste, or group. People could not change the caste into which they were born.

CASTES IN ANCIENT INDIA

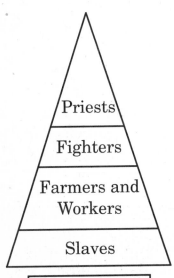

Priests

Fighters

Farmers and Workers

Slaves

Outcastes

Look at the chart on this page. You can see that some castes were higher, or more important, than other castes. The highest caste included the priests. In a caste lower than the slaves were the outcastes. The outcastes had to do the jobs that no one else wanted to do.

The caste system has lasted for thousands of years. The government of India made parts of the caste system illegal in the 1900s.

The Aryans also brought with them their beliefs about gods and goddesses. These beliefs became a religion called **Hinduism**. Hinduism is still followed by many people in India today.

One important belief of Hinduism is that people are born again in different bodies after they die. People who lead a good life are rewarded in the next life. For example, a kind and hardworking farmer might be born again as a priest. But people who are lazy or cruel might be sorry. They might be born again as outcastes. In Hinduism, it's important to lead a good life.

➤ **In what way were Hindu beliefs about what happens after a person dies the same as ancient Egyptian beliefs?**

_____

_____

_____

Chinese Civilization

Like the story of Indian civilization, the story of Chinese civilization goes back thousands of years. It began in the Huang He valley. The first Chinese were farmers, and the valley they lived in was a fertile one. Each summer the Huang He flooded. Like the Sumerians and the Egyptians, the Chinese irrigated their farms.

The Chinese learned to work together. About 4,000 years ago, they began to live in villages and cities. About the same time, a powerful family named Shang united all the villages and cities in the Huang He valley. This ruling family became known as a **dynasty**. In a dynasty, when a king dies, his oldest son becomes the new king. The Chinese were ruled by one dynasty after another until the early 1900s.

The Han Dynasty began about 2,000 years ago. China became strong and rich during the Han Dynasty. The Han family conquered many new lands. They also built a wall to protect their new land. This wall is called the Great Wall of China. The Great Wall still stands today. It is thousands of miles long and took many years to build.

The Great Wall of China is the longest wall in the world.

➤ **Look at the picture. In what kind of land region was this part of the Great Wall built?**

Mysterious Bones

About 100 years ago, an exciting discovery was made in the Huang He valley of China. Farmers at work in their fields found some mysterious animal bones. The bones had strange marks and cracks on them.

Archaeologists studied the bones. They realized that the marks and cracks were thousands of years old. They showed the earliest writing in China. How had the bones been used? People scratched pictures on the bones and heated them until they cracked. Then they would read the pictures and cracks to tell what would happen in the future.

The Chinese language today does not have an alphabet like English does. Instead of 26 letters, there are thousands of different symbols, or characters.

A Man of Peace

Around 2,500 years ago, a man was born who would become one of China's great teachers. He was called Confucius. His ideas influenced Chinese government and society for over 2,000 years. He taught a way of life that helped bring about peace and a just government.

Little is known about the early life of Confucius. He is supposed to have been a good student. When he was still a young man, Confucius became a government worker. Later, he became a teacher. There was much warfare and bad government when he lived. He traveled all over China, trying to teach government workers the best way to govern.

Confucius felt that there could be no peace until people learned to live good and kind lives. You have read that China was ruled by one family after another. The family was very important in Chinese culture. Confucius believed that peace and justice began in the family. He taught that children should respect their parents. He also taught that parents should respect their children.

Confucius believed there were five virtues, or qualities, that people must have:

- They must want to do good to one another.
- They must act kindly toward one another.
- They must honor and respect one another.
- They must try to get learning and knowledge.
- They must be sincere.

Confucius used these ideas when he talked to China's rulers. He taught that rulers should be wise and kind. In return, people should obey their rulers.

➤ **Write one rule you would make to help people lead good lives. Explain why.**

_____

_____

_____

_____

_____

Chapter Checkup ✓

➤ **Darken the circle by the answer that best completes each sentence.**

1. Indian civilization began in
   - Ⓐ the Fertile Crescent.
   - Ⓑ the Nile River valley.
   - Ⓒ the Huang He valley.
   - Ⓓ the Indus River valley.

2. Chinese civilization began in
   - Ⓐ the Fertile Crescent.
   - Ⓑ the Nile River valley.
   - Ⓒ the Huang He valley.
   - Ⓓ the Indus River valley.

3. One important belief of Hinduism is that
   - Ⓐ there is one god.
   - Ⓑ people can tell what will happen in the future.
   - Ⓒ people can do whatever they want.
   - Ⓓ people are born again after they die.

4. The highest caste in Indian society included the
   - Ⓐ priests.
   - Ⓑ fighters.
   - Ⓒ farmers.
   - Ⓓ outcastes.

5. Chinese writing has
   - Ⓐ 26 letters.
   - Ⓑ 26 characters.
   - Ⓒ letters written on bones.
   - Ⓓ thousands of characters.

6. Confucius thought that
   - Ⓐ China was a powerful country.
   - Ⓑ people could tell what would happen in the future.
   - Ⓒ rulers should do anything they want to do.
   - Ⓓ people must honor and respect one another.

Thinking & Writing

How were the ancient civilizations described in this chapter alike? How were they different? Explain your answer.

_____

_____

_____

_____

_____

_____

_____

CHAPTER 7 — Ancient Africa

You have already read about ancient Egypt, the first civilization in Africa. Egypt is located in northern Africa. This area is separated from the rest of Africa by a huge desert called the Sahara.

South of the Sahara, the land and climate of Africa are different. In some areas there are thick rain forests. Elsewhere, there are grassy plains that remind some visitors of the Great Plains in the United States.

Africa is the birthplace of humanity. Many scientists believe that humankind first began and developed in Africa. The ruined city called Zimbabwe or Great Zimbabwe is believed by some archaeologists to be the biblical site of Ophir, where King Solomon's mines were located. The city was occupied at different times by different peoples. About a thousand years ago, the city was surrounded by a great wall. Inside the wall, people built richly decorated buildings.

➤ **What other civilizations that you have read about built walls around their cities?**

_____

Africa is also famous for its long history. You may remember that Egypt was conquered by other kingdoms. Some of those kingdoms were found in Africa. In this chapter, you will read about some of those African kingdoms.

A traditional house in Zimbabwe

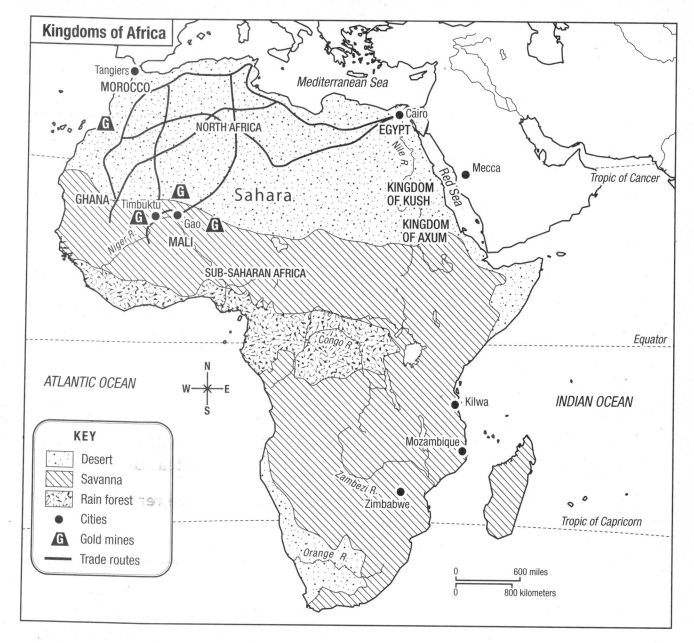

Kingdoms of Africa

- Tangiers
- MOROCCO
- Mediterranean Sea
- NORTH AFRICA
- Cairo
- EGYPT
- Mecca
- Nile R.
- Red Sea
- Tropic of Cancer
- GHANA
- Sahara
- KINGDOM OF KUSH
- Timbuktu
- KINGDOM OF AXUM
- Gao
- MALI
- Niger R.
- SUB-SAHARAN AFRICA
- Congo R.
- Equator
- ATLANTIC OCEAN
- N W E S
- Kilwa
- INDIAN OCEAN
- Mozambique
- Zambezi R.
- Zimbabwe
- Orange R.
- Tropic of Capricorn

KEY
- Desert
- Savanna
- Rain forest
- ● Cities
- G Gold mines
- — Trade routes

0   600 miles
0   800 kilometers

The Cave Painters

Look at the map on this page. Land south of the Sahara is called sub-Saharan Africa. The grasslands of Africa are called the **savanna**.

➤ **Use a colored pencil to trace the borders of both the Sahara and the savanna.**

Thousands of years ago, the Sahara had a different climate. It rained often, and plants, animals, and people lived there. Archaeologists know this because hundreds of cave paintings of these things have been found in the Sahara.

The Ancient Kingdom of Kush

More than 2,000 years ago, an African king named Piankhi traveled down the Nile with his army and defeated Egypt. For hundreds of years after this, the Kingdom of Kush was the most important civilization in Africa.

Kush was located just south of Egypt. In fact, the people of Kush had learned a great deal from the Egyptians. For example, they learned how to write Egyptian hieroglyphics and how to build pyramids. But the pyramids of Kush were somewhat different.

The capital of Kush was a beautiful city called Meroe. Once, a visitor to Meroe wrote that the people of Kush were good at making iron tools. But one thing amazed this visitor—the streets of the city were filled with elephants!

The people of Kush used elephants for an important purpose. These animals carried iron tools and gold to faraway places. There the people of Kush traded tools and gold for precious jewelry and rare glass. The people of Kush were some of the first traders. They traveled great distances on their elephants.

The Rise of Axum

Kush was surrounded by powerful neighbors. Kush was located south of Egypt. To the south of Kush was a land called Ethiopia. Axum was the most important city in Ethiopia. About 1,700 years ago, the people of Axum conquered and destroyed the city of Meroe.

Stories say that the king who conquered the people of Meroe was very proud. He had the story of his conquest carved on a tall stone column. He wrote that he had burned the houses of Kush and carried away its food, iron, and gold. Whatever was worthless, his soldiers had thrown into the Nile.

Axum soon became a great trading city. People sailed their boats from Asia to ports along the Ethiopian coast. They came to trade clothing and jewels for gold, ivory, and other African riches. A visitor from Asia described the wealth and beauty of the king's court in Axum. He said that the king rode through the streets of his city in a golden chariot that was pulled by painted elephants.

➤ **Name two ways in which the culture of Axum was like the culture of Kush.**

_____

_____

The Kingdoms of West Africa

Far to the west of Kush and Ethiopia, another kingdom began to grow about 1,800 years ago. The ruler of this new kingdom was known as *ghana*, which means "king of the gold." Later, the word *ghana* was used as the name for his kingdom.

"King of the gold" was a good name for this ruler. South of Ghana, in hills near the city of Timbuktu, there was much gold. The leaders of Ghana knew exactly where the gold could be found, but they kept it a secret. Traders from North Africa and Egypt, looking for gold, crossed the endless miles of the Sahara to come to Ghana.

These traders passed through desert salt mines on their way west. They strapped blocks of the salt on their camels. Then, after a six-month journey, the traders arrived in the country ruled by the "king of the gold." They traded large blocks of salt for the gold.

This may seem like an unfair trade, but it wasn't. Salt is necessary for human life. It is used to keep food from spoiling. The people of Ghana did not have salt, so they were willing to trade gold to get it.

Ghana remained strong for almost 800 years. Then warriors from the north invaded Ghana and took over the gold trade. As you will see, however, West African civilization would continue to grow.

➤ **Why are resources like gold important to growing civilizations like Ghana?**

_____

_____

The Empire of Mali

The warriors from the north who conquered Ghana came from a kingdom called Mali. *Mali* means "where the king lives."

A great ruler came to power in Mali over 700 years ago. Under this king, Mansa Musa, Mali became a center of learning, as well as a rich kingdom.

In 1324, Mansa Musa set out to visit Egypt. He traveled in a **caravan**. A caravan is a group of people and animals that travel together. Out of the blowing sands of the Sahara, Mansa Musa appeared in Egypt with thousands of travelers from Mali. His camels were loaded down with hundreds of pounds of gold.

While he was in Egypt, the king invited teachers to Timbuktu in Mali. Like Meroe and Axum, Timbuktu first became important as a trading city in Ghana. Under Mansa Musa, however, Timbuktu also turned into a city where learning was very important. People came to study history and law.

➤ **Look at the map on page 47 and circle Timbuktu.**

As you have read, we know about many of these African kingdoms today because travelers wrote about their visits. Some of these kingdoms, such as Axum and Ghana, had no written language. But they developed interesting cultures based on trade.

Chapter Checkup ✓

➤ **Darken the circle by the answer that best completes each sentence.**

1. Archaeologists know that people lived in the Sahara thousands of years ago because
   Ⓐ the desert is a good place to grow crops.
   Ⓑ gold could be found there.
   Ⓒ cave paintings have been found in the Sahara.
   Ⓓ ancient cities have been found in the Sahara.

2. The people of Kush tamed elephants to
   Ⓐ carry salt.
   Ⓑ carry tools and gold to faraway places.
   Ⓒ make iron tools.
   Ⓓ build pyramids.

3. Asian traders came to Axum to trade for
   Ⓐ clothes and elephants.
   Ⓑ gold and ivory.
   Ⓒ salt and pepper.
   Ⓓ caravans.

4. The people of Ghana traded gold for
   Ⓐ water.
   Ⓑ silver.
   Ⓒ ivory.
   Ⓓ salt.

5. In a caravan, people travel together with
   Ⓐ cars.
   Ⓑ elephants.
   Ⓒ gold.
   Ⓓ animals.

6. Under Mansa Musa, the kingdom of Mali became
   Ⓐ a caravan.
   Ⓑ a center for learning.
   Ⓒ the capital of Ethiopia.
   Ⓓ part of Egypt.

Write about one way that the ancient kingdoms of Africa are like the civilizations of Mesopotamia, China, or India. Write about one way in which they are different.

_____

_____

_____

_____

Unit 2 📋 Skill Builder Comparing Distance Scales

Sometimes a map has a smaller map called an inset map that shows part of the larger map in more detail. The two maps have different distance scales. Look at the maps below.

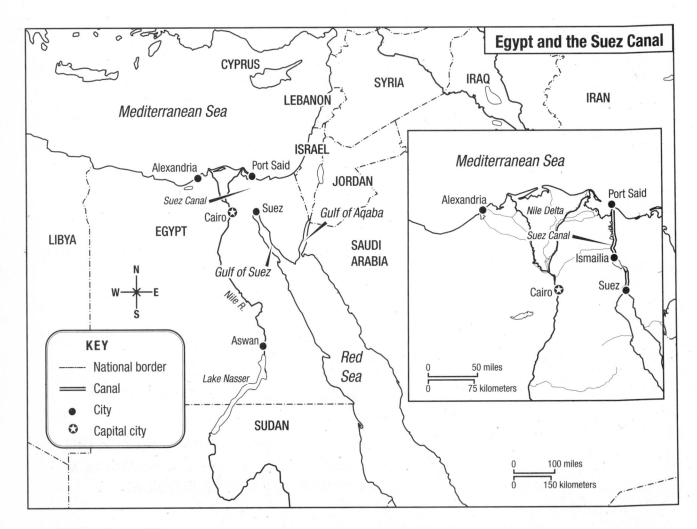

1. What is the distance in miles from Cairo to Aswan?

_____

2. Which map would you use to find the distance between Cairo and Ismailia? What is the distance in kilometers?

_____

3. Measure the distance between Alexandria and Cairo on the two maps. Write the distance in miles here.

_____

Unit 2 Test

➤ **Darken the circle by the answer that best completes each sentence.**

1. The two rivers that run through Mesopotamia are the Tigris and the
   Ⓐ Nile.
   Ⓑ Euphrates.
   Ⓒ Canaan.
   Ⓓ Hammurabi.

2. The person who led the Hebrews out of slavery in Egypt was
   Ⓐ Moses.
   Ⓑ Hammurabi.
   Ⓒ Tutankhamen.
   Ⓓ Aryan.

3. The ruler of Egypt was called the
   Ⓐ papyrus.
   Ⓑ mummy.
   Ⓒ pharaoh.
   Ⓓ hieroglyphic.

4. An ancient city on the Indus River in India was called
   Ⓐ Huang He.
   Ⓑ Mohenjo-Daro.
   Ⓒ Aryan.
   Ⓓ Hindu.

5. A great Chinese teacher was named
   Ⓐ Confucius.
   Ⓑ Huang He.
   Ⓒ Mohenjo-Daro.
   Ⓓ Sumer.

6. The city of Meroe was the capital of
   Ⓐ Axum.
   Ⓑ Timbuktu.
   Ⓒ Kush.
   Ⓓ Ghana.

Thinking & Writing

Think about the civilizations that you have read about in this unit. Imagine that you are the ruler of a civilization. Like Moses and Hammurabi, create a set of laws for your civilization.

_____

_____

_____

_____

_____

_____

_____

_____

CHAPTER 8 Classical Greece

Greek civilization was very different from the civilizations that grew up in the river valleys of Egypt and Mesopotamia. For one thing, Greece had very little good farmland. Yet, in one way, Greece was very much like ancient Egypt. Life in Egypt depended on the Nile River. Life in ancient Greece also depended on a body of water—the sea.

▶ **Look at the map on page 55. Name the seas the Greeks would have depended on.**

_____

_____

Life in ancient Greece centered on the Aegean Sea. Look at the map again. You can see that the Aegean Sea is near the eastern end of the Mediterranean Sea. Greece is surrounded by sea on three sides. The ancient Greeks depended on the sea for food. And sea travel was easier than trying to cross tall mountains and plateaus. In this chapter, you will read how important the sea was to ancient Greek civilization.

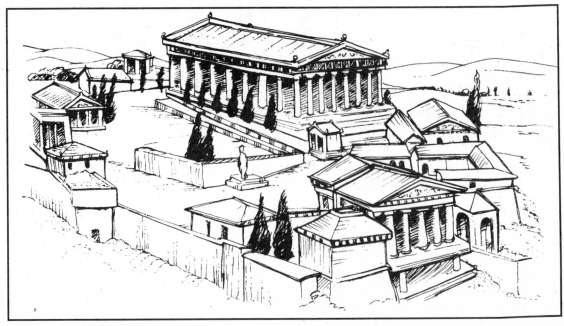

The Acropolis in ancient Athens

A Civilization Shaped by the Sea

Greek farmers could not grow enough food to feed everyone in Greece. So the Greeks needed to find other resources to meet their needs. They became sailors and traders. They built special ships. Strong rowers and large sails made these ships travel fast. Over time, Greek ships could travel all over the Aegean and Mediterranean Seas. They carried resources from other places back to Greece.

Greek traders and their ships soon became an everyday sight in Egypt and Mesopotamia. The Greeks brought with them grapes, wine, olives, wool, and pottery. The Greeks used these goods to trade with people in other places. In Mesopotamia and Egypt, the Greeks traded for meat, lumber, and vegetables. When their ships were full, the Greeks sailed for home.

But the Greeks received more than food from their neighbors. They learned how to make better tools and how to build faster ships. After all, when Greek civilization was just beginning 3,000 years ago, the Egyptian civilization was already 2,000 years old. Soon the Greeks became richer and stronger. They set up **colonies** around the Aegean world. A colony is an area of land controlled by another country or parent state.

➤ **Look at the map below. Circle the areas that were controlled by Greece almost 2,500 years ago.**

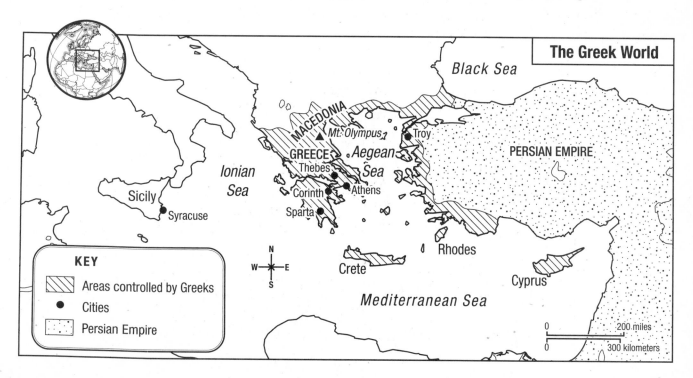

Beginning of the City-States

The ancient Greeks built a civilization very different from the civilization of Egypt. The pharaoh ruled over all the cities in Egypt. The ancient Greeks built city-states. Each city-state was independent and had its own ruler.

The Greeks built city-states all over the Aegean. Two city-states, however, soon became richer and more powerful than the rest. These city-states were called Sparta and Athens.

Sparta

Sparta was located in southern Greece. The Spartans had the best army in Greece. They did not become rich by trading, but by conquering other city-states. The people they conquered became slaves in Sparta.

Life in Sparta was controlled by the army. Children were raised to be strong and useful to the city-state. At the age of about seven, boys were taken away from their parents. They were raised in special camps. There they learned to use weapons. They learned to follow orders. Everything was done to turn the boys into strong soldiers.

Spartan girls were also trained to defend the city-state. They played sports and grew strong. When they grew up, they ran farms and businesses while their husbands went to war.

➤ **Unlike other cities and countries, Sparta did not have a wall around its city. A person who lived in Sparta once said, "Every Spartan is a brick in the wall around Sparta." What do you think this person meant?**

_____

Athens

Sparta may have been the strongest Greek city-state. But Athens was larger and richer. It was located on the Aegean Sea. Ships sailed in and out of Athens every day. Traders brought news from all over the world to the Athenians, or the people of Athens. As a result, new ideas were always welcome in the city. The Athenians trained their children to be good students, athletes, and **citizens**. A citizen is a person who is a member of a country, either by birth or by choice.

One of the most important places in Athens was the **agora**. This was the biggest marketplace in the city. It was also the busiest part of the city. Shops, temples, and government buildings were all found near the agora. People came from Mesopotamia, Egypt, and other Greek city-states to sell their goods. Cloth, pottery, and jewelry were sold. Tables were piled high with bread, fish, cheese, and vegetables.

The people of Athens came to the agora to shop, but they also came to talk and to listen. Teachers met there with students. People talked about the government. People were able to talk about the government because Athens was a **democracy**. This means that the people made their own laws. Athens was not ruled by a king.

Athens was not the kind of democracy we have today. Only men who had been born in Athens could vote. No women could vote. Men who had been born in other cities could not vote. Greek democracy was not perfect, but it was a powerful new idea. Later civilizations have borrowed the idea and added to it.

➤ **Name ways in which Sparta and Athens differed in how they raised their sons.**

_____

_____

The Acropolis

On a hill high above the agora and the rest of Athens stood the Acropolis. The Acropolis was made up of many buildings. The Athenians met there to talk about important business. The picture on page 54 shows what the Acropolis looked like. The largest building on the Acropolis was called the Parthenon. The Parthenon was a temple. There the Athenians honored the goddess Athena. Athena was the Greek goddess of wisdom. The Athenians believed that Athena protected their city.

Ruins of the Parthenon

Socrates

Statue of Socrates

Athens had many great writers, artists, and wise people. One of the wisest people in Athens was Socrates. Almost everyone in Athens knew him. This is because Socrates could always be found in the agora, asking questions.

Socrates was famous for asking questions about almost everything. What, he asked, was the meaning of truth? How do people decide what is right and wrong? Socrates asked many questions, but he did not give many answers. He wanted the people of Athens to think for themselves. Some Athenians did not like this. They thought Socrates taught people to question too much. They sentenced Socrates to death.

A student of Socrates named Plato continued to teach the ideas of Socrates. Plato wrote down these ideas. Then he set up the world's first university. It lasted for many years, and the ideas of Socrates spread. Even today, people still study Socrates by reading the writings of Plato.

Theater

The Greeks loved to see plays. Some of the first plays for the theater were written in Greece. The Greeks watched plays in outdoor theaters. Sitting on stone seats, they sometimes stayed all day and watched one play after another. Plays that had a sad ending were called **tragedies**. Plays that ended happily were **comedies**.

The Olympic Games

Have you ever seen the Olympic Games on television? Did you know that they were first played in ancient Greece? Every four years, athletes ran races, wrestled, and jumped over high fences. The winner received a crown of olive leaves. Success in the games was a great honor for the ancient Greeks.

You have read a lot about the civilization of Greece in this chapter. The Greeks were interested in ideas and sports. They built the world's first democracy. Many later civilizations learned much from the ancient Greeks.

➤ **How often were the Olympic Games held in ancient Greece?**

Chapter Checkup ✓

➤ **Darken the circle by the answer that best completes each sentence.**

1. Ancient Greece was made up of
   Ⓐ river valleys.
   Ⓑ mountainous regions.
   Ⓒ good farmland.
   Ⓓ land in Asia and Africa.

2. An important resource for the Greeks was
   Ⓐ the sea.
   Ⓑ gold.
   Ⓒ lumber.
   Ⓓ farmland.

3. Greek city-states were
   Ⓐ cities that were part of a nation.
   Ⓑ independent and had their own rules.
   Ⓒ cities that did not have governments.
   Ⓓ cities built on islands.

4. Athens was different from Sparta because
   Ⓐ it was more warlike than Sparta.
   Ⓑ it was not a city-state.
   Ⓒ it was ruled by a king.
   Ⓓ it was larger and richer.

5. Socrates taught his students to
   Ⓐ find the truth by thinking for themselves.
   Ⓑ shop in the agora.
   Ⓒ destroy the city-states.
   Ⓓ never ask questions.

6. The Olympic Games were
   Ⓐ plays that the Greeks watched all day.
   Ⓑ held to honor Socrates.
   Ⓒ contests for athletes.
   Ⓓ held once a week.

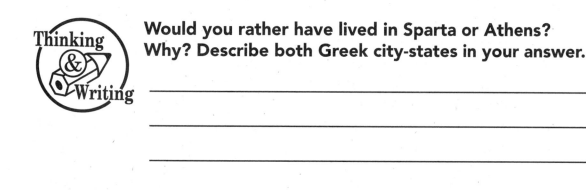

Thinking & Writing

Would you rather have lived in Sparta or Athens? Why? Describe both Greek city-states in your answer.

_____

_____

_____

_____

_____

_____

CHAPTER

9 The Roman Empire

The ideas of Greece helped shape another great civilization—the civilization of Rome. "All roads lead to Rome" was a common saying in ancient times. It meant that the city of Rome was the center of a large **empire**. An empire is a large area of land with many different people. It is controlled by one person or a small group.

But Rome did not become an empire overnight. It began as a small village on the Tiber River in Italy about 2,700 years ago. Italy has many mountains and hills, like Greece. Unlike Greece, it also has good farmland. The first Romans were farmers.

➤ **Look at the map on page 61. Use the distance scale to find the distance in miles from Athens to Rome.**

The Colosseum was built in the center of Rome.

An Unusual Beginning

The ancient Romans liked to tell a story about how Rome began. Once there were twin baby brothers named Romulus and Remus. A cruel uncle left them to die in the Tiber River. A mother wolf found the babies. She protected them. Romulus and Remus grew up to start Rome on the shores of the Tiber River.

This story shows that the Romans, like the twins who grew up in the wilderness, thought of themselves as strong and brave.

➤ **Look at the map below. Tell in what direction each of the following places was from Rome: London, Carthage, the Danube River, and Egypt.**

_____

_____

The Early Republic

At first, Rome was ruled by kings. Many kings were cruel. About 2,500 years ago, the Romans decided they did not want to be ruled by kings anymore.

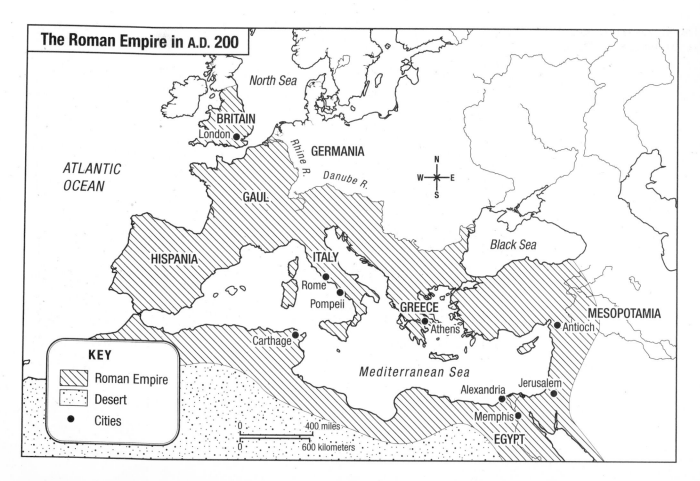

The Romans set up a **republic**. In a republic, the people have the right to choose their own leaders. You may remember that in Athens all male citizens could vote. But in the Roman Republic, some men had more power than others. Rich men were called **patricians**. The common people of Rome were called **plebeians**. Only patricians could become leaders in the new Roman Republic.

Rome Begins to Grow

After Rome became a republic, the Romans built a strong army. They began to take over more land in Italy. Some people did not like this. The people of Carthage, for example, wanted to stop Rome. Carthage was a rich trading city in North Africa. Both Rome and Carthage wanted to control trade in the Mediterranean. Soon Carthage was at war with Rome.

A general from Carthage named Hannibal surprised the Romans. He attacked Rome from the north instead of by sea. To do this, he had to make a dangerous journey across the Alps. His army rode through the mountains on elephants. Imagine a soldier coming up against an elephant in battle!

➤ **Look at the map on page 61. How many miles is Carthage from Rome?**

**A painting of
Julius Caesar**

The Roman Empire

Carthage and Rome fought long and hard for 15 years. Finally, the Romans won the war. Soon Rome controlled parts of what are now Spain, France, Greece, and North Africa.

Julius Caesar

As Rome conquered more territories, its government changed. People no longer chose their rulers. Instead, Rome was ruled by **dictators**, or rulers who have total power. Many of these dictators were generals. They became powerful because they conquered new lands for Rome. One of the most famous Roman dictators was Julius Caesar.

Caesar conquered many new lands for Rome. But the people of Rome were getting tired of war. Caesar promised to keep Rome out of new wars.

Caesar was popular among many poor people. He promised to find jobs for them. However, some Roman patricians did not trust Caesar. They thought he wanted too much power. They were afraid that he would try to make himself king. For this reason, they killed Caesar.

➤ **Why do you think some Romans were afraid of being ruled by a king again?**

_____

_____

Augustus Caesar

After Caesar's death, the Roman Republic came to an end. Rome was governed by Caesar's grandnephew. He took the name Augustus Caesar. *Augustus* means "respected one."

Augustus became the first **emperor** of Rome. An emperor is a person who rules an empire. Augustus ruled well for 41 years. He made sure that Rome and its empire were ruled fairly. He also built many monuments, theaters, and other buildings in Rome. Augustus liked to say, "I found Rome brick and left it marble."

Under Augustus, a period of peace began in the Roman Empire. This peace lasted for almost 200 years. It was called the **Pax Romana**, which means "Roman peace."

The Roman army protected all the people in the empire. Roman soldiers built forts on the borders of the empire. They fought to keep the empire safe from people who lived outside the empire.

The Birth of Christianity

Palestine was a land in the Roman Empire. Palestine was the Roman name for Canaan. When Augustus ruled, a man who changed world history was born in Palestine. His name was Jesus. The parents of Jesus were Mary and Joseph.

Jesus became a teacher. He taught that there was only one god. He said that the people must honor God by treating others with love and kindness. Like Moses, he told people they should follow the Ten Commandments.

Many people began to follow the teachings of Jesus. But some people did not like what Jesus taught. People in the Roman government thought Jesus was trying to turn people against Rome. They sentenced Jesus to death.

The followers of Jesus created a new religion— **Christianity**. The death of Jesus did not put an end to his teachings. But the government tried to stop Christianity from spreading. They did not like Christianity because Christians refused to worship Roman gods and refused to serve in the army.

➤ **In what way were Judaism and Christianity different from other religions in the ancient world?**

_____

_____

B.C.

3100	– Menes unites all Egypt
2590	– Work on the Great Pyramid begins
2000	– High point of Sumerian civilization
1790	– Hammurabi becomes king of Babylon
1025	– Saul becomes king of Palestine
800	– Greek city-states begin to form
776	– First Olympic Games held
753	– Rome founded
470	– Birth of Socrates
461	– Golden Age of Greece begins
450	– Roman law written
312	– Work on first Roman road begins
270	– Rome dominates all of central Italy
63	– Rome conquers Palestine
– 0 –	**Birth of Jesus**
167	– First outsiders invade Italy
200	– Persecution of Christians begins
313	– Constantine ends persecution of Christians
476	– Roman Empire in West falls to invaders

A.D.

The Romans killed many Christians. They made practicing Christianity against the law. But the number of Christians continued to grow. Finally, the Roman emperor Constantine made Christianity **legal**, or lawful, in the Roman Empire.

How Old Is It?

The birth of Jesus was an important event in world history. Today, many people in the world measure all dates from this date. The birth of Jesus divides our calendar into two parts.

The years before Jesus's birth are marked B.C. These initials stand for "before Christ." The years following the birth of Jesus are marked A.D. This stands for "Anno Domini." Anno Domini means "Year of Our Lord" in Latin, the language of ancient Rome. Remember, B.C. dates increase backward. For example, the year before 1 B.C. is 2 B.C. The year before 2 B.C. is 3 B.C., and so on. Like ordinary numbers, A.D. dates increase forward. For instance, after the year 2007 comes the year 2008.

Look at the time line on this page. Use the time line to answer the following questions.

➤ **How many years before Jesus was born were the first Olympic Games held?**

_____

How many years passed between the date when the Olympic Games were first held and the date when work on the first Roman road began?

_____

How many centuries passed between the birth of Jesus and the date when Constantine ended the persecution of Christians?

_____

How many years passed between the time that Greek city-states began to form and the persecution of Christians began?

_____

Chapter Checkup ✔

➤ **Darken the circle by the answer that best completes each sentence.**

1. The city of Rome is in
   - Ⓐ Greece.
   - Ⓑ Egypt.
   - Ⓒ North Africa.
   - Ⓓ Italy.

2. The first Roman government was called
   - Ⓐ a dictatorship.
   - Ⓑ a republic.
   - Ⓒ an empire.
   - Ⓓ a civilization.

3. A group of Roman patricians killed Julius Caesar because
   - Ⓐ they wanted to rule themselves.
   - Ⓑ they wanted to overthrow the Roman Empire.
   - Ⓒ they thought he was a weak ruler.
   - Ⓓ they feared he would make himself king.

4. Augustus Caesar was
   - Ⓐ a dictator before Julius Caesar.
   - Ⓑ a plebeian.
   - Ⓒ the first Roman emperor.
   - Ⓓ a Christian leader.

5. The Pax Romana was
   - Ⓐ a long period of peace throughout the Roman Empire.
   - Ⓑ a war between Rome and Carthage.
   - Ⓒ an important building in Rome.
   - Ⓓ a powerful Roman emperor.

6. Jesus taught that
   - Ⓐ people should fight for the Roman Empire.
   - Ⓑ he was the ruler of Rome.
   - Ⓒ people should treat one another with love.
   - Ⓓ people should worship Roman gods.

Thinking & Writing

Compare Julius Caesar or Augustus Caesar with another ruler you have read about, such as Hammurabi or Mansa Musa.

_____

_____

_____

_____

_____

_____

_____

The Middle Ages

The Roman Empire lasted for more than a thousand years. Over time, however, the empire began to grow weak. There were many reasons this happened. Some emperors were cruel and dishonest. Warriors from the north attacked the borders of the empire.

In A.D. 476, warriors finally captured the city of Rome. The mighty Roman Empire had come to an end. In this chapter, you will read about a new time in the history of Europe that began then.

➤ **Name two ways the Roman Empire brought civilization to many parts of Europe.**

_____

_____

The Early Middle Ages

The years between the fall of Rome and A.D. 1500 are now called the Middle Ages. This means they are a time "in between." Before the Middle Ages, there were the civilizations of Greece and Rome. After the Middle Ages, modern nations existed.

The early years of the Middle Ages were the hardest for people. Many leaders fought one another for power and land. The signs of civilization that Rome had brought to Europe began to crumble away. Trade began to disappear because fierce warriors from the north still roamed through the countryside. They destroyed crops and robbed homes and farms.

Notre Dame Cathedral in Paris

www.harcourtschoolsupply.com
© Harcourt Achieve Inc. All rights reserved.

67

Unit 3, Chapter 10
Core Skills Social Studies 6, SV 9781419039058

The Feudal System

KING

HIGHER NOBLES
(vassals to king;
have knights)

LOWER NOBLES
(vassals to higher
nobles; have knights)

COMMON PEOPLE
(may become
serfs to nobles)

The Rise of Feudalism

Finally a system developed that brought order to Europe. It was called **feudalism**. Feudalism was a kind of government. It was also a way of life. Under feudalism, powerful people agreed to protect those who were less powerful. The chart on this page shows how feudalism worked.

The king gave land to the **nobles** under him. The nobles were rich men from the upper class. In return for the land, the nobles promised to help fight the king's enemies. The nobles were called **vassals** of the king. Sometimes a noble gave some of his land to another noble, who then became his vassal. Vassals who fought for their king or for other nobles were called **knights**. Only men were knights during the Middle Ages.

The people listed in the lower part of the chart were the common people. Many were **serfs**. A serf was someone who farmed the land. Serfs had to pay rent and taxes to the nobles, and they were not allowed to move away without permission. In return, the nobles protected the serfs from attack.

➤ **Look at the chart. In what way were higher nobles and lower nobles the same?**

Daily Life Under Feudalism

Most people in the early Middle Ages lived on a **manor**. A manor included the noble's house, a small village, a church, a mill, and fields and woods. Since trade had almost died out, a manor had to grow or make many things people needed to live. Clothing, for example, was made of wool from the sheep raised on the manor. Carpenters worked on buildings, while other workers made tools.

➤ **What jobs would you have wanted to do if you had lived on a manor?**

The noble's house was often a fort or castle with thick stone walls. It was usually a cold, drafty place. The noble, his wife, and their children lived in this huge building. The servants and skilled workers of the manor lived there, too. Some of the noble's knights also lived there. They protected the noble and his family from attack.

The serfs lived in the village. Their huts were usually made of sticks and mud. In case of attack, the serfs raced to get inside the castle.

The serfs had to do many jobs for the noble's family. The men cut wood and farmed. The women worked in the castle as cooks and servants. In return, the noble gave the serfs protection and places to live.

Christianity in the Middle Ages

A small church was an important part of each manor. By the year A.D. 1000, most of the people of Western Europe were Christians. At this time, all Christians were members of the Roman Catholic Church. Over time, the church replaced the power of Rome as something that kept people together.

For example, the church saved education from completely disappearing after the fall of Rome. Christian priests learned to read and write Latin, which became the language of the church. Sometimes they taught others how to read and write, but there weren't many educated people. And all books were handwritten! Even kings and queens sometimes did not know how to read and write. There was almost no chance for a serf to learn how to read.

The church also helped keep the knowledge of Greece and Rome from being forgotten. At that time, the only way to copy a book was to write it by hand. There were no printing presses or copy machines. Religious men and women called **monks** and **nuns** copied hundreds of books by hand. Without the church, much of our knowledge of the ancient world would have been lost.

Many noble families lived in a castle.

A crusader

The church was very important during the Middle Ages. Many large, beautiful churches called **cathedrals** were built. Cathedrals were among the greatest works of art of the Middle Ages. Artists brought scenes from the Bible to life in shining windows of colored glass. Wood and stone carvings decorated the inside and the outside.

Everyone became involved in the building of the cathedrals. Nobles helped pay for them. The common people helped build them.

The Crusades

During the Middle Ages, most people did not travel far from the manor where they lived. But some Christians made a long, difficult journey. They went to visit the city of Jerusalem. Christians thought that Jerusalem was a holy city because Jesus had lived there.

In the Middle Ages, Jerusalem was ruled by people who followed a religion called Islam. The followers of Islam are known as **Muslims**. You will read more about Islam later in this book.

Around A.D. 1000, Muslims in Jerusalem no longer welcomed Christian visitors. When this happened, the **pope** told the Christians of Europe to go to Jerusalem. The pope was the leader of the Roman Catholic Church. He said it was their duty to free Jerusalem from the power of the Muslims.

The Christians went on several journeys to try to capture Jerusalem. These journeys were called the **Crusades**. The Christians fought battles with the Muslims and captured the city of Jerusalem in 1099. However, about 100 years later, the Muslims won it back.

➤ **Why do you think visiting Jerusalem was important to a Christian in the Middle Ages?**

_____

_____

The Growth of Towns and Cities

The Crusades changed Europe in many important ways. To reach Jerusalem, the crusaders had to travel far. Crusaders who returned brought treasures home with them. They brought silks, rugs, and jewels, as well as foods that Europeans had never seen before—lemons, rice, and sweet, juicy oranges. The Europeans wanted more. Soon a busy trade began between Europe and the East.

➤ **Look at the map below. Use your pencil to trace the route of the first Crusade.**

Slowly, trade among the countries of Europe began to grow, too. Roads were rebuilt. People began to move from manors to towns. People who worked at certain jobs formed groups called **guilds**. There were many guilds. Shoemakers had a guild, for example. So did bakers and weavers. Soon many Europeans became more interested not just in the East, but in their own past—the civilizations of Greece and Rome.

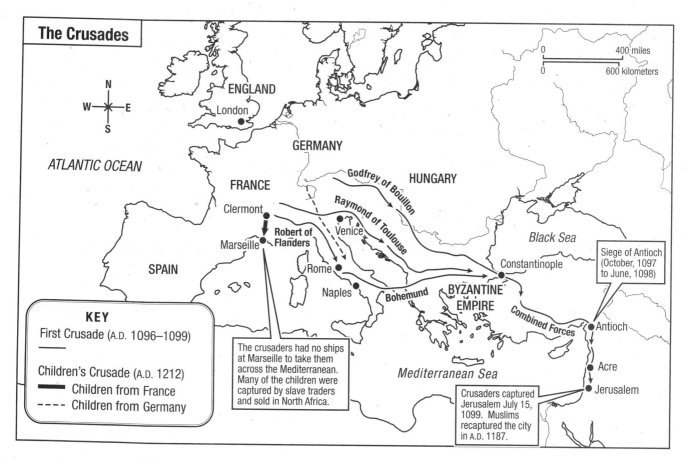

71

Chapter Checkup ✓

➤ **Darken the circle by the answer that best completes each sentence.**

1. The term *Middle Ages* means
   Ⓐ a "time in between."
   Ⓑ the fall of Rome.
   Ⓒ an age when serfs stopped working.
   Ⓓ the years between A.D. 50 and 150.

2. Feudalism was
   Ⓐ a city in Western Europe.
   Ⓑ a series of wars.
   Ⓒ a system that brought order and safety to Europe.
   Ⓓ a crusade to win control of Jerusalem.

3. A knight was
   Ⓐ a warrior.
   Ⓑ a priest.
   Ⓒ the ruler of an empire.
   Ⓓ a member of a guild.

4. Serfs lived
   Ⓐ in castles.
   Ⓑ in huts on the manor of a noble.
   Ⓒ in large cities.
   Ⓓ in guilds so they could learn a trade.

5. The Christian church helped
   Ⓐ serfs get permission to leave their manor.
   Ⓑ divide Europe.
   Ⓒ destroy learning.
   Ⓓ keep alive the learning of Greece and Rome.

6. The Crusades were
   Ⓐ journeys to try to capture Jerusalem from the Muslims.
   Ⓑ large churches that were built by nobles and serfs.
   Ⓒ a ruling family.
   Ⓓ treasures brought back to Europe from Jerusalem.

Thinking & Writing

What were some of the ways that the Roman Catholic Church helped keep education from disappearing during the Middle Ages? Why was this important?

_____

_____

_____

_____

_____

_____

CHAPTER 11 Early Modern Europe

Leonardo da Vinci's
Mona Lisa

In the 1300s, Francesco Petrarch, an Italian poet, wrote these words: "Do not forget the ancient Greeks and Romans. . . . The ancient books are welcome friends. . . ."

Petrarch was not the only person in the 1300s who looked to the Greeks and Romans for answers. Europe was changing. As you have read, the Crusades brought Europeans together with people from the East. Trade increased and towns began to grow. As people traded, they exchanged ideas. In this chapter, you will see how the Europeans developed new ideas by looking back at their own past.

➤ **In what early civilization did an increase in trade lead to the spread of new ideas?**

The Renaissance

There was a period of change in Europe after the Crusades. We call that time the Renaissance. *Renaissance* is a French word that means "rebirth."

During the Renaissance, people developed new ideas about literature, art, and science. Renaissance artists admired the work of Greek and Latin artists. But as they looked to the past, they also began to develop new ideas.

Michelangelo was one of the greatest artists of this period. Leonardo da Vinci was another great artist. When he was very young, Leonardo wrote, "I wish to work a miracle." In his lifetime, he created many "miracles." One of them was the painting called *Mona Lisa*. Leonardo also studied science. He kept a notebook filled with new ideas for inventions.

Michelangelo, Leonardo, and Petrarch were just three of the artists and thinkers during the Renaissance. There were many others. Suddenly, it did not seem important if a person was a serf. What a person could do became more important.

➤ **Why is the term *Renaissance*, or "rebirth," a good name for this time in Europe?**

The Pieta by
Michelangelo

Martin Luther

The Reformation

In 1517, the ideas of another Renaissance thinker, Martin Luther, changed European history forever. Luther was a monk who had developed some new ideas about Christianity. He became angry at the Roman Catholic Church. You may remember that the Roman Catholic Church was the only church during the Middle Ages. The pope was the head of the church. What had the church done to make Luther angry?

Luther was angry because the pope would forgive people for their mistakes if they gave money to the church. In other words, if you did something against the teachings of the church, you could pay money and be forgiven. Luther thought this was wrong.

In 1517, Luther nailed a list of 95 of his beliefs to a cathedral door in Wittenberg, Germany. Church leaders were very angry. They told Luther he could no longer belong to the church. However, some people thought Luther was right.

Luther's ideas spread quickly. The invention of the printing press around 1450 helped make this possible. With a printing press, what had taken days to copy by hand could be printed in minutes! All across Europe, people began to read about Luther's beliefs.

Luther left the Roman Catholic Church in 1520. Many people followed him. Luther's followers became known as **Protestants**. This is because they "protested" against Roman Catholic practices. In time, the movement begun by Luther became known as the Reformation. In 1545, reforms, or changes, were also made in the Catholic Church.

➤ **Why was the printing press an important invention?**

_____

_____

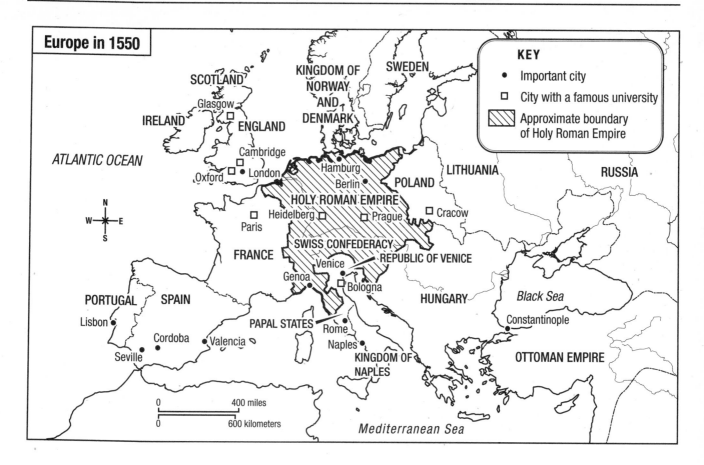

A New Europe

As towns grew during the Renaissance, the feudal system began to grow weak. Under feudalism, kings were really no more powerful than nobles. Now, with taxes from growing towns, some kings became very powerful. They were able to raise armies and control large areas of land.

During the 1500s and 1600s, more people began to think of themselves not as serfs or the citizens of a town. They began to think of themselves as members of a nation. A **nation** is a large group of people who share the same language, history, government, and culture. The kings who formed these nations set up systems of laws to govern them.

➤ **Spain, France, and England were among the first nations in Europe. Look at the map on this page. The city of Rome was not a part of a nation in the year 1550. Where was Rome located?**

King John signing the Magna Carta

The First Nation in Europe

In A.D. 1066, a nobleman named William sailed from his home on the coast of France. He led a great army that quickly conquered the English. On Christmas Day in 1066, William was crowned King of England.

William was a strong king. After he died, other kings built a strong government for England. In the 1100s, a king named Henry II set up laws for all of England. Because these laws applied to everyone, they were called **common law**.

But the English people never thought that kings should have total power over the people. In 1215, English nobles forced King John to sign a paper called the **Magna Carta**. *Magna Carta* means "great charter" in Latin. The Magna Carta limited the power of the king. It showed that even the king was governed by English common law. By the end of the 1400s, the nation of England was strong and united.

➤ **In what way is English common law the same as laws we have in the United States today?**

_____

_____

The Industrial Revolution

Throughout the 1500s and 1600s, England continued to grow and gain power. Soon England had become one of the world's major trading nations. Its major **product** was **textiles**, or cloth. At the time, most of England's textiles were made by women in their homes. But more and more people wanted English cloth. England began to look for faster ways to make textiles.

Imagine that you make cloth in England in the 1700s. People around the world want to buy your cloth. But you can't make enough cloth for everyone. What will you do? You could get more people to help you make cloth. You could invent machines to help you do the work. Both these things happened in England in the 1700s.

These machines included the steam engine and the spinning jenny, which helped one person do the work of many. These inventions, both in the 1760s, were important in the development of the cotton textile industry. Coal mines were expanded to provide power for the growing textile factories.

New machines and industries made a great change in how people lived. This time is now called the **Industrial Revolution**. Before the Industrial Revolution, most of England's people lived on farms. After the Industrial Revolution, most people lived where factories were located—in towns and cities. In time, the revolution that started in England spread to other parts of Europe and to the United States.

➤ **The world *revolution* means "a great change in the way people think and live." How does this describe the Industrial Revolution?**

_____

_____

During the Industrial Revolution, working conditions were often poor. As more factories were built, more people were needed to work in them. Many children worked long hours on machines.

Over the next hundred years, most nations in Europe developed great industries based on steel, coal, and oil. So did the United States. These industries brought money and power to western nations. The Industrial Revolution changed the way people lived in these nations forever.

Chapter Checkup ✓

➤ **Darken the circle by the answer that best completes each sentence.**

1. The growth of trade during the Middle Ages led to
   Ⓐ the fall of Rome.
   Ⓑ the growth of feudalism.
   Ⓒ the Crusades.
   Ⓓ the growth of towns.

2. During the Renaissance, thinkers and artists looked back to the civilization(s) of
   Ⓐ Egypt.
   Ⓑ Mesopotamia.
   Ⓒ Greece and Rome.
   Ⓓ India and China.

3. The Reformation was a time when
   Ⓐ changes were made in the Roman Catholic Church.
   Ⓑ people began to make goods in factories.
   Ⓒ people made lifelike paintings and sculptures.
   Ⓓ cathedrals were built throughout Europe.

4. Martin Luther was told to leave the Roman Catholic Church for
   Ⓐ painting the *Mona Lisa*.
   Ⓑ inventing the spinning jenny.
   Ⓒ questioning the power of the church.
   Ⓓ telling people to study the civilizations of Greece and Rome.

5. As kings became more powerful in Europe, they
   Ⓐ formed new nations with strong governments.
   Ⓑ built feudal manors.
   Ⓒ built Protestant churches.
   Ⓓ left Europe to fight in the Crusades.

6. The Industrial Revolution was made possible by
   Ⓐ the growth of towns.
   Ⓑ the invention of new machines.
   Ⓒ Martin Luther.
   Ⓓ Michelangelo and Leonardo da Vinci.

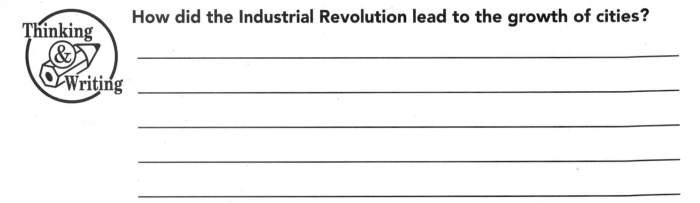

Thinking & Writing

How did the Industrial Revolution lead to the growth of cities?

_____

_____

_____

_____

_____

78

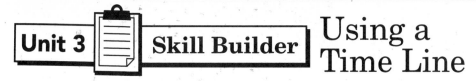

Unit 3 | **Skill Builder** | Using a Time Line

Look at the time line below. This time line covers the Middle Ages, the Renaissance, the Reformation, and the early years of the Industrial Revolution. A lot happened during all those years!

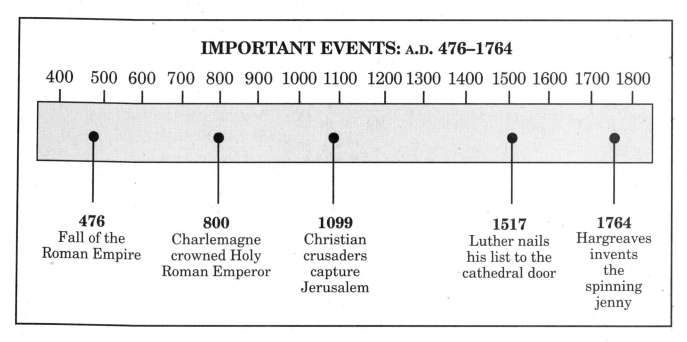

IMPORTANT EVENTS: A.D. 476–1764

400 500 600 700 800 900 1000 1100 1200 1300 1400 1500 1600 1700 1800

476
Fall of the
Roman Empire

800
Charlemagne
crowned Holy
Roman Emperor

1099
Christian
crusaders
capture
Jerusalem

1517
Luther nails
his list to the
cathedral door

1764
Hargreaves
invents
the
spinning
jenny

1. What happened in 476?

_____

2. When did Charlemagne become Emperor of the Holy Roman Empire?

_____

3. The Muslims recaptured Jerusalem in 1187. Mark the date on the time line and write a label for the event.

4. How many years went by between Charlemagne being crowned emperor and Luther nailing his list to the cathedral door?

_____

5. The years between the fall of Rome and the year 1500 are called the Middle Ages. Think of a way of showing the Middle Ages time period on the time line. Write your idea on the time line.

Unit 3  Test

➤ **Darken the circle by the answer that best completes each sentence.**

1. The people of Athens, not the king, made the laws because Athens was
   - (A) a city-state.
   - (B) an agora.
   - (C) communist.
   - (D) a democracy.

2. Life in Sparta was controlled by the
   - (A) army.
   - (B) children.
   - (C) slaves.
   - (D) marketplace.

3. Julius Caesar was a Roman
   - (A) king.
   - (B) Christian.
   - (C) dictator.
   - (D) plebeian.

4. The general from Carthage who crossed the Alps with elephants was
   - (A) Augustus Caesar.
   - (B) Hannibal.
   - (C) Julius Caesar.
   - (D) Romulus.

5. The wars the Christians fought against the Muslims to recapture Jerusalem were called
   - (A) the Crusades.
   - (B) feudalism.
   - (C) guilds.
   - (D) cathedrals.

6. Martin Luther has come to be known as the leader of the
   - (A) Renaissance.
   - (B) Industrial Revolution.
   - (C) Reformation.
   - (D) Middle Ages.

During which time period would you like to have lived, the Renaissance or the Industrial Revolution? Explain your answer.

_____

_____

_____

_____

_____

_____

_____

_____

Name _____   Date _____

CHAPTER 12

The Eastern Hemisphere: Geography and Climate

You have been reading about different places in the world. It is important to learn where places are. With a few facts, you can find any place on a map or globe.

The equator is an imaginary line drawn on maps and globes. The equator runs east to west. It divides the world into two **hemispheres**. The Northern Hemisphere is the half that is north of the equator. The Southern Hemisphere is the half south of the equator.

The **prime meridian** also divides the world into two hemispheres. The Eastern Hemisphere is the half of the world east of the prime meridian. The Western Hemisphere is the half of the world west of the prime meridian. In this chapter, we will take a closer look at the geography and climate of the Eastern Hemisphere.

➤ **Use your pencil to circle the United States on the map below. Is the United States in the Eastern or Western Hemisphere?**

_____

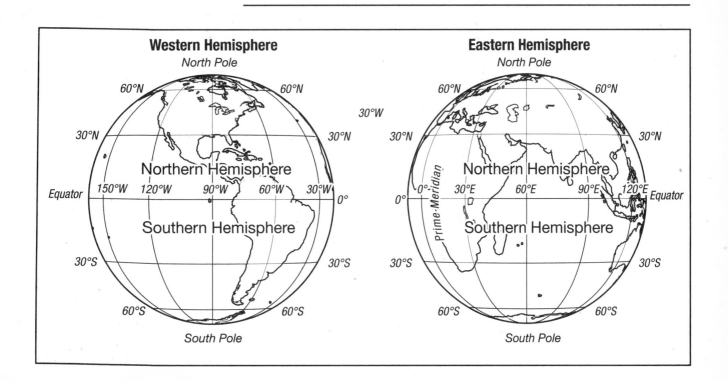

Latitude and Longitude

Parallels, also called **lines of latitude**, run east and west. Meridians, also called **lines of longitude**, run north and south. When both parallels and meridians are drawn on a map or globe, they form a **grid**. A grid is a pattern that looks like a net. You can find any place if you know its parallel and its meridian. The parallel is always named first. For example, Ankara, on the map below, is at 40°N, 33°E. That means it is on the 40th parallel, or latitude, north of the equator, and the 33rd meridian east of the prime meridian.

➤ **What city is at 35°N, 90°W?**

_____

On what meridian, or line of longitude, is the city of London?

_____

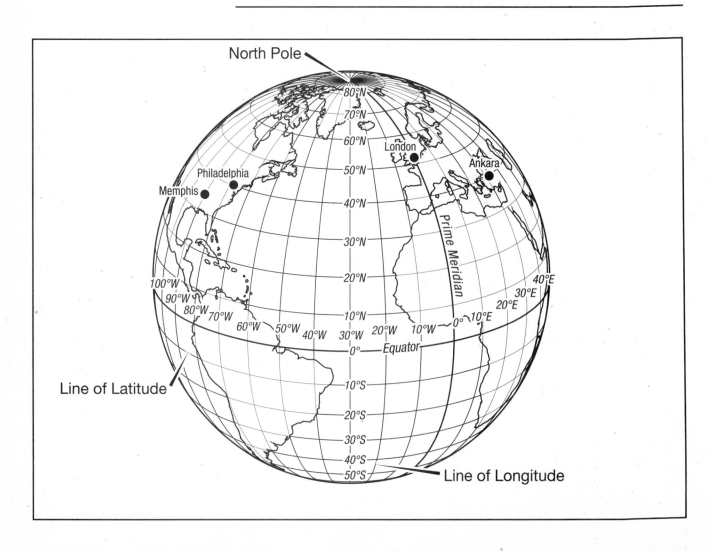

Europe

Europe is one of the smallest continents in the world. Only Australia is smaller. Yet Europe has more people than any other continent except Asia. One reason for this is that a large plain stretches through Europe, from the Atlantic Ocean to Asia. It is called the North European Plain, or the Great European Plain. It has some of the best farmland in the world.

➤ **Why would most people want to live in an area with good farmland?**

_____

_____

Along the southern border of the North European Plain lie rugged mountains. The most famous mountains in Europe are the Alps. They are known for their snowy beauty. Europe has many rivers, and many of them begin in the Alps. Europe's rivers are major routes of transportation.

The ocean is another major route of transportation for the nations of Europe. There is no place in Europe that is more than a few hundred miles from the Atlantic Ocean. Europe is a **peninsula**, which means it is surrounded on three sides by water. The nearness of the ocean and the sea have helped shape Europe's history. Many famous explorers came from Europe. And, as you remember, both the Greeks and the Romans were excellent sailors.

The Atlantic Ocean also has a great effect on Europe's climate. Many places in northern Europe are mild, even though they are far north. This is because they are kept warm by breezes from a mild ocean **current** called the Gulf Stream. Currents are like rivers that flow through oceans. The Gulf Stream is a warm current because it starts at the equator.

➤ **How might the nearness of the ocean and sea have shaped European civilization?**

_____

_____

The Matterhorn is the most familiar mountain in the Alps.

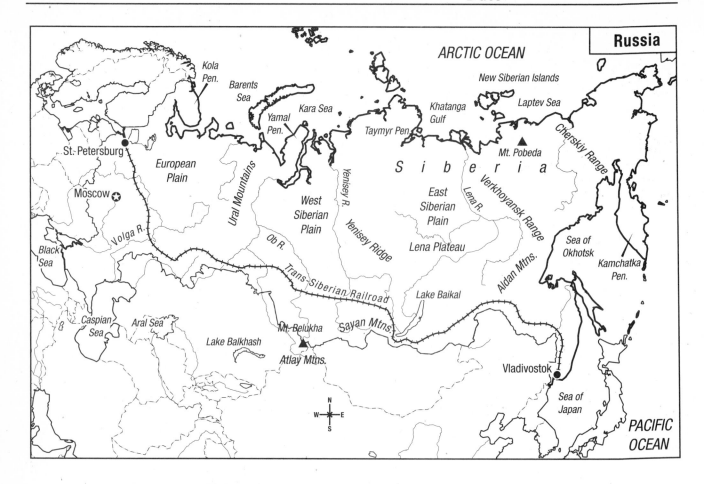

Russia

Russia is the largest country in the world. It stretches across Europe and Asia. Part of Russia is called European Russia, and part is called Asian Russia.

There are no rivers that connect European Russia and Asian Russia. So railroads became a popular form of transportation. Today, you can take a trip by train across Russia.

Your trip would begin in the city of St. Petersburg, one of the busy cities of European Russia. As you look out the train window, you pass wide fields and forests. After a long while, however, your train slowly begins to climb up into the rocky Ural Mountains. The Ural Mountains divide Europe from Asia.

The landscape and climate of Russia change as you travel. In Russia's far north, where it is bitterly cold, only tiny plants can grow. This area is called the **tundra**.

➤ **Your train trip ends in Vladivostok, a city in Asian Russia. Circle Vladivostok on the map above.**

Mount Everest in the Himalayas

South Asia

You may remember that the ancient city of Mohenjo-Daro is located in the Indus River valley. Look at the map on page 40 and locate the Indus River valley.

Some of the highest mountains in the world can be found just north of here. One of South Asia's largest mountain ranges is called the Himalayas. The Himalayas rise along China's southwest border with India, Nepal, and Bhutan. The highest mountain in the world, Mount Everest, is part of the Himalayas.

➤ **This area of South Asia is sometimes called "the roof of the world." Why is that a good name?**

_____

South Asia's geography, however, includes more than just mountains. You have already read about the rich plain where Mohenjo-Daro was built. This fertile valley lies south of the Himalaya Mountains. The mighty rivers that irrigate the soil there begin in the Himalayas.

Still farther south is a great peninsula that makes up the country of India. Much of this peninsula is covered with short grasses. The soil has been baked dry by the hot sun. Even some of the rivers there have dried up.

At the very tip of the peninsula of South Asia, the climate changes. Here it rains often. The soil and the forests at the tip of South Asia produce valuable goods such as pepper and wood.

The climate of South Asia changes with the seasons. These changes are very important to South Asia's farmers. The climate depends on special winds that are called **monsoons**. The monsoons blow from different directions at different times of the year. From November to March, the monsoons bring dry air. From April through October, they bring heavy rains. The farmers know they can depend on rain and dry weather at certain times for their crops.

North Africa

You have already read about the Nile River valley. But this valley is only a small part of North Africa. Every continent except Europe has deserts. However, North Africa is unusual because so much of it is covered by desert. In fact, the largest desert in the world is found in North Africa. It is called the Sahara.

A desert is a place that has very little rainfall—less than ten inches a year! It is also a place where the soil is very dry. Most deserts are found in warm climates. The climate of North Africa is one of the hottest and driest in the world.

Because the soil is dry, very few plants and animals can live there. But people have lived in the desert for many centuries. Most of them live near an **oasis**. An oasis is an underground spring in the desert. There are more than 90 large springs and many smaller ones in the Sahara. Villages have grown up near many of them.

Much of the Sahara is covered by sand dunes, which are hills of sand. But other parts are made up of rocky plateaus. Since there are few plants to hold the soil in place, there is erosion. In the Sahara, winds blow the sand from place to place.

➤ **Look at the picture below. Why do you think some people call the Sahara a "sea of sand"?**

The Sahara

The Variety of the Eastern Hemisphere

You have read about rich farmland and dry deserts, towering mountains and wide plains. In the chapters to come, you will read about the people who live in the Eastern Hemisphere today.

Chapter Checkup ✓

➤ **Darken the circle by the answer that best completes each sentence.**

1. The prime meridian divides the world into
   - Ⓐ parallel lines.
   - Ⓑ the Eastern and Western Hemispheres.
   - Ⓒ the Northeastern and Southern Hemispheres.
   - Ⓓ a grid.

2. The Eastern Hemisphere includes
   - Ⓐ Europe.
   - Ⓑ Canada.
   - Ⓒ the United States.
   - Ⓓ Mexico.

3. Europe's climate is
   - Ⓐ tropical.
   - Ⓑ largely a desert.
   - Ⓒ freezing cold everywhere.
   - Ⓓ affected by the ocean and sea.

4. Russia
   - Ⓐ has a long Atlantic coast.
   - Ⓑ stretches across Asia and Europe.
   - Ⓒ is the smallest continent.
   - Ⓓ is the smallest country.

5. Monsoons are
   - Ⓐ mountains.
   - Ⓑ lakes.
   - Ⓒ countries in South Asia.
   - Ⓓ winds in South Asia.

6. Much of the Sahara is covered by
   - Ⓐ grass.
   - Ⓑ water.
   - Ⓒ sand dunes.
   - Ⓓ plants.

Thinking & Writing

How is the geography of South Asia different from the geography of North Africa?

_____

_____

_____

_____

_____

_____

_____

CHAPTER 13 Europe

Diplomats in San Francisco, 1945

It is May 1945. In the city of San Francisco, California, cheers can be heard coming from the Opera House on Van Ness Avenue. But there are no singers on stage. Instead, **diplomats** from 50 nations are clapping. A diplomat is a person who works to handle business between his or her nation and other nations. These diplomats had a good reason to clap. They had just made a plan for a new world group— the United Nations.

World War II had ended in Europe in May. The leaders of many nations wanted to find a way to stop future wars. They thought that if the nations of the world could talk and work together, peace might be possible. They also wanted to find a way to help nations fight sickness and hunger.

➤ **Brainstorm some ways in which nations might help one another.**

_____

_____

It wasn't long before the United States and the Soviet Union declared a different kind of war. In this chapter, you will read about the Soviet Union and Europe and about how Soviet power ended.

The Spread of Communism

At the end of World War II, the Soviet Union was the strongest nation in Europe. But about 20 million Soviet citizens and soldiers died in the war. Joseph Stalin was the Soviet leader. He wanted to make sure that the Soviet Union would never be attacked again. He also wanted to spread **communism**. Communism is a form of government in which everything is owned by the government. The people cannot choose their leaders.

President Truman asking Congress to help Western Europe oppose communism

Before the United Nations meeting in San Francisco, Stalin agreed to let the people of Eastern Europe choose their leaders. However, Stalin did not keep the agreement. He wanted the Eastern European nations to become communist.

➤ **Look at the map below. Circle the names of the European nations that bordered the Soviet Union.**

By 1947, U.S. President Harry Truman thought Stalin and the Soviets had to be stopped. But the nations of Western Europe had just fought a war. They were not strong enough to stand up to the Soviets. So Truman said the United States would help.

With American help, the nations of Western Europe did become strong again. At the same time, the Soviets strengthened their control over Eastern Europe. By 1948, communist governments ruled in Poland, Czechoslovakia, Bulgaria, Romania, and Hungary. Albania and Yugoslavia were also communist, but they were not under Soviet control. Europe was now divided into two **blocs**, or parts. They were the Soviet bloc and the Western bloc.

➤ **Which bloc did France and Great Britain belong to after World War II?**

_____

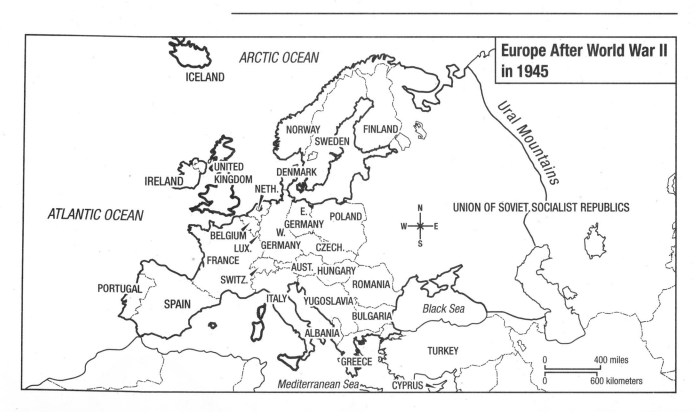

Europe After World War II in 1945

The Cold War

The trouble between the East and the West became known as the Cold War. A **cold war** is not a war that people fight with weapons. The nations involved in a cold war do not trust each other.

After Germany lost World War II, the United States, France, Great Britain, and the Soviet Union divided Germany into four zones, or areas. In 1948, the United States, France, and Great Britain decided to rejoin their three zones into one country. The country became known as West Germany. It was a democracy.

The Soviet Union, however, did not allow its zone to join with the rest of Germany. Instead, a separate country called East Germany was formed. It had a communist government, like the Soviet Union. So Germany was divided into two nations.

The city of Berlin was an unusual city in Germany. Berlin was in East Germany, but it was split into two halves. One half was controlled by the Communists. The other half was a Western democracy. Between 1948 and 1961, almost three million people crossed from East Berlin into West Berlin to escape communism. In an effort to stop this, the East German government built a wall dividing East and West Berlin in 1961. Any person trying to cross the Berlin Wall was shot by guards.

➤ **Why did East Germany build the Berlin Wall?**

_____

_____

The Berlin Wall

Protesting Communism

Throughout the 1940s and 1950s, the nations of Western Europe slowly rebuilt their homes, roads, and factories. The nations of Eastern Europe did not do as well. Compared to the nations of Western Europe, the nations of Eastern Europe remained poor. When Eastern Europeans protested against communism, they were often put in jail.

In 1956, people in Hungary protested for more freedom. But Soviet tanks moved in to stop the protest. In 1968, the people in Czechoslovakia wanted to change their government, too. Once again the Soviets moved in. The Communists stayed in power.

In the 1970s, the people of Poland tried many times to win more freedom from their communist government. In 1981, Poland's workers formed a **union** called Solidarity. A union is a group of workers who get together for a special reason. The people who belonged to Solidarity had a special reason. They wanted higher pay and free elections in Poland.

A man named Lech Walesa was the leader of Solidarity. He led shipyard workers in the city of Gdansk, Poland, on a **strike**. In a strike, people refuse to work until they get what they want. But then the Soviet-backed government in Poland stopped the strike. The government ruled that it was against the law for people to strike. But Polish workers continued to fight for changes. In 1989, Poland had a new government. The Communists were no longer in control.

News of the changes in Poland's government soon reached the other nations of Eastern Europe. Throughout 1989, one nation after another asked for democracy and an end to communism. In 1989, parts of the Berlin Wall were taken down so people from East and West Germany could move between the two countries. By 1991, communism had ended in Eastern Europe. East and West Germany were reunited. The Cold War was almost over.

➤ **Why did workers in Poland form a special union?**

_____

_____

The Fall of Communism

Why, after 40 years, did the Soviet Union suddenly allow noncommunist governments in Eastern Europe? Many people think Soviet leader Mikhail Gorbachev was responsible.

When Gorbachev became the Soviet leader in 1985, the Soviet Union faced many problems. The economy was in trouble. People wanted more freedom. Gorbachev knew that something had to be done. He thought that the Cold War was one of the Soviet Union's biggest problems.

The Soviet Union spent huge amounts of money on soldiers and weapons to keep communist governments in Eastern Europe. So much money was spent that the Soviet people were poor. In 1987, Gorbachev decided to spend less money on weapons. At the same time he announced a new plan called **glasnost**. *Glasnost* means "openness," or "more freedom." But by 1992, the people had grown tired of communist rule. They voted Gorbachev and the Communists out of power. The Cold War was over. The Soviet Union became 15 separate nations. The largest of these are Russia, Kazakhstan, and Ukraine.

➤ **Circle the names of the three largest nations that were once part of the Soviet Union. Why did the Soviet people end communism?**

_____

_____

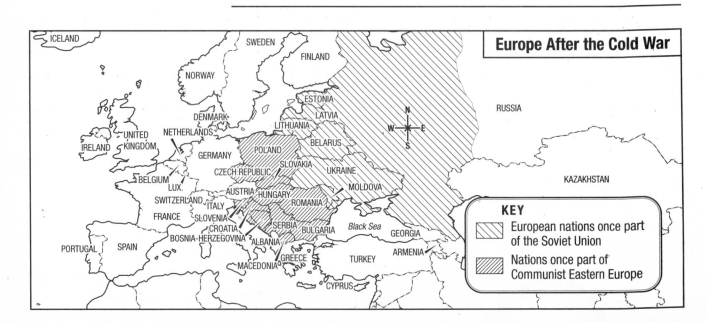

Europe After the Cold War

KEY
- European nations once part of the Soviet Union
- Nations once part of Communist Eastern Europe

Russia Today

Following the fall of communism, Boris Yeltsin replaced Gorbachev. But instead of being the head of the Soviet Union, Yeltsin became the president of Russia. Russia is the largest and most powerful of the republics that made up the former Soviet Union. The end of a communist form of government caused major political and economic change in Russia.

Instead of just one political party—the Communist Party—there were many political parties. By 1995, more than 40 political parties participated in an election.

Under communism, all businesses were owned and controlled by the government. The Russian government sold government-owned businesses to private citizens. Citizens were also allowed to start their own businesses. The Russian government hoped that these changes would help the Russian economy get stronger.

At first, though, there was economic hardship. At the end of 1999, Boris Yeltsin resigned. Vladimir Putin was elected president of Russia in 2000. Early in this century, the Russian economy began to recover.

But Russia still faces problems. Some groups within Russia want independence from Russia. In 1994, Russia became involved in a war in Chechnya. Chechnya is an area of Russia. Chechnya wants to become its own nation and not be part of Russia. Russian army troops and Chechen soldiers have fought many bloody battles. In 2006, the issue had still not been resolved.

➤ **What changes occurred in Russia after the fall of communism?**

Chapter Checkup ✓

➤ **Darken the circle by the answer that best completes each sentence.**

1. The United Nations was started in 1945 to
   Ⓐ find a way to stop future wars.
   Ⓑ end World War II.
   Ⓒ begin the Cold War.
   Ⓓ build an opera house in San Francisco.

2. Under communism, all land and businesses are
   Ⓐ owned by the members of Solidarity.
   Ⓑ owned by the president.
   Ⓒ owned by the government.
   Ⓓ owned by the United States.

3. President Truman wanted to keep Europe strong so that it could
   Ⓐ build a wall between East and West Germany.
   Ⓑ protect the United States in war.
   Ⓒ stand up to the Soviet Union and stop the spread of communism.
   Ⓓ start communist governments in the Western Hemisphere.

4. During a cold war,
   Ⓐ the Soviet Union and Eastern Europe fight.
   Ⓑ some nations do not trust each other.
   Ⓒ people fight each other with weapons.
   Ⓓ communism is spread around the world.

5. The Communists built the Berlin Wall to keep
   Ⓐ West Germans out of Eastern Europe.
   Ⓑ workers in Poland from forming a union.
   Ⓒ Americans from visiting the Soviet Union.
   Ⓓ East Germans from escaping to West Germany.

6. By 1991, the Soviet Union had
   Ⓐ elected a new communist leader.
   Ⓑ won the Cold War against the United States.
   Ⓒ broken up into 15 separate nations and ended communism.
   Ⓓ sent Soviet troops into Poland and Romania.

Thinking & Writing

Why did Mikhail Gorbachev want to end the Cold War?

_____

_____

_____

CHAPTER 14 Africa

In the 1300s and 1400s, Europeans had heard stories about the people who lived on the huge continent of Africa. But the first Europeans who came to Africa did not really know what to expect.

European explorers and traders brought news of Africa back to Europe. They talked of a continent that had great resources. Soon many Europeans were coming to Africa with plans to become rich. In this chapter, you will read how Africans later gained their **independence**, or freedom, from Europe.

➤ **How did Europeans find out about the resources of Africa?**

_____

_____

Natural resources help the economy of many African countries.

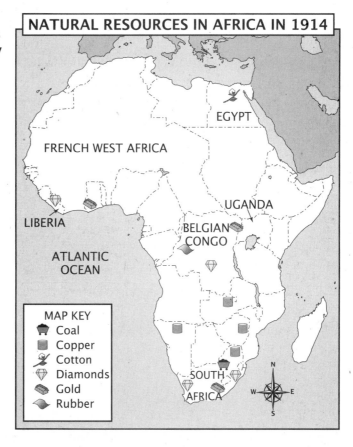

NATURAL RESOURCES IN AFRICA IN 1914

The Slave Trade

At first, Africa was important to Europe for only one reason. Goods from Africa could be traded in Asia. The Europeans sent ships filled with cloth and tools along the African coast. They returned to Europe with gold and ivory. The growth of colonies in North and South America, however, changed trade in Africa.

Beginning in the late 1400s, many European nations claimed lands in North and South America. They built large farms there, called **plantations**. Sugar cane, cotton, fruits, and coffee grew on the plantations. Many people were needed to work there. Soon the Europeans were traveling to Africa for something besides gold. They wanted slaves.

Europeans hired slave catchers to take people from African villages. These slave catchers were usually sailors who rowed ashore and hid. Then they seized Africans who wandered nearby. Some slave catchers were Africans who were paid to capture other Africans for the slave trade. The prisoners were crowded onto large ships. Then they were sent on a long voyage to the Americas.

➤ **Think about the civilizations you have read about. Which of these civilizations had slaves?**

Slave trader leading slaves

The journey on a slave ship was terrible. Many people were packed closely together and had no room to move. One in six Africans died during the trip. Many more died after they were sold into slavery in the Americas.

By the late 1700s, about 70,000 people were taken from Africa every year to become slaves. A total of about 12 million slaves were sold before the slave trade ended around 1870.

Results of the Slave Trade

The slave trade in Africa harmed everyone. Families were broken apart. Tens of thousands of people died. Those who lived found themselves in a strange land, unable to leave. In Africa, many villages were almost destroyed by the slave trade. Few young people were left to care for the land and to start families.

The slave trade also affected Europeans. Many Europeans began to think they were better than the Africans. This kind of thinking led to **racism**. Racism is the belief that people of some races are better than people of other races. Racism has been the cause of many problems in many countries around the world.

➤ **Why do you think so many Africans died on board slave ships?**

_____

_____

Slave dealer auctioning off slaves

Growth of Imperialism

The populations of European countries were increasing very quickly in the 1800s. The Industrial Revolution had started. Africa was important to Europeans because of its resources.

Many European countries began to follow a policy called **imperialism**. Imperialism is the control of the economy and government of one country by another.

➤ **Look at the map. Which European countries still had colonies in Africa in 1951?**

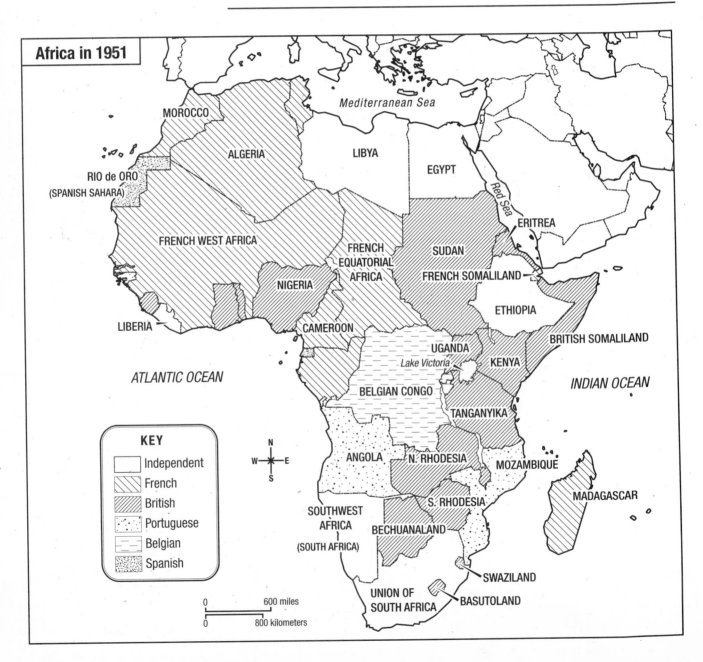

Africa in 1951

KEY
- Independent
- French
- British
- Portuguese
- Belgian
- Spanish

Name _____ Date _____

Results of European Imperialism

The European countries that ruled Africa did not know or care much about the Africans. The borders between colonies often separated groups that had always lived together. Other groups that had been at war for centuries were forced to live in one nation.

Most Africans lived under European rule for over 100 years. Africans did not have success in their fight for independence until after World War II.

➤ **Look at the map below and the map on page 98. What nations were made from French Equatorial Africa?**

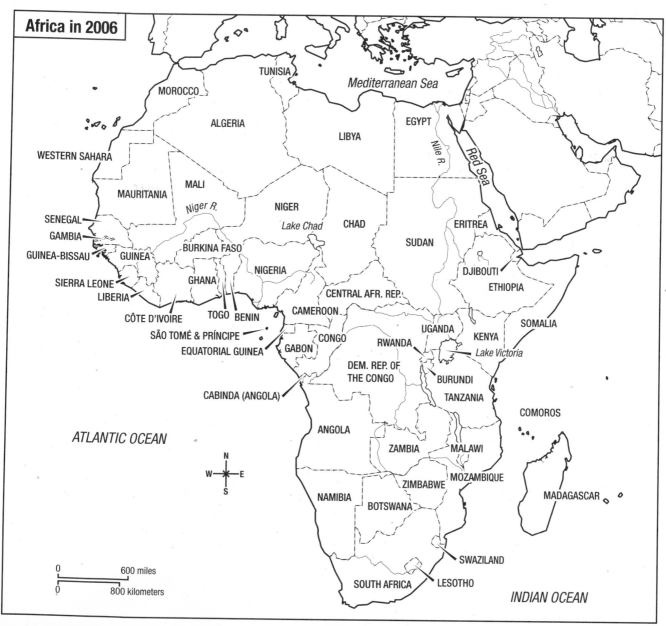

Independence Movements

The first African nation to become independent was Ghana. Ghana's first leader was Kwame Nkrumah. Nkrumah led a movement known as Self-Government NOW. The members of Self-Government NOW led **boycotts** against the European governments. During a boycott, people refuse to buy goods produced by another group or government. Boycotts can hurt a nation's economy. Then the government sometimes gives the people what they want. Boycotts helped the people of Ghana win independence on March 6, 1957.

▶ **What was one way the people of Ghana used to win independence?**

_____

_____

Some African nations did not get their independence peacefully. Many people were killed when Kenya tried to win its freedom from Great Britain. One of the leaders of Kenya's independence movement was Jomo Kenyatta. In December 1963, Kenya became independent. The people of Kenya chose Jomo Kenyatta to be the nation's first leader. Cries of "Uhuru! Uhuru!" could be heard throughout Nairobi, the capital of Kenya. *Uhuru* is a Swahili word that means "freedom."

Nigeria was another African country that won its freedom from Great Britain in the 1960s. Today, Nigeria has been helped by the discovery of oil. The money earned from selling oil helps Nigerians develop their nation.

Other countries in Africa that have gained independence include Zimbabwe, Zambia, Mozambique, Burundi, and Eritrea.

Nairobi, the capital of Kenya

Name _____ Date _____

Chapter Checkup ✓

➤ **Darken the circle by the answer that best completes each sentence.**

1. European nations wanted slaves to
   Ⓐ work on European sailing ships.
   Ⓑ work on plantations in the Americas.
   Ⓒ work in factories in Europe.
   Ⓓ build European ships.

2. The slave trade harmed people because
   Ⓐ it put an end to racism all over the world.
   Ⓑ Africans were separated from their families.
   Ⓒ Europeans became lazy.
   Ⓓ people in Asia did not want slaves.

3. Imperialism is
   Ⓐ the control of the economy and government of one country by another.
   Ⓑ an African independence movement.
   Ⓒ a system of government in Ghana today.
   Ⓓ a boycott against a government.

4. Most African nations became independent
   Ⓐ in the 1700s.
   Ⓑ before World War II.
   Ⓒ after World War II.
   Ⓓ in the 1980s.

5. During a boycott,
   Ⓐ many people get killed.
   Ⓑ people buy goods from another government.
   Ⓒ people refuse to buy goods produced by another group.
   Ⓓ a leader is elected.

6. The first leader of Kenya was
   Ⓐ Nelson Mandela.
   Ⓑ a European.
   Ⓒ Kwame Nkrumah.
   Ⓓ Jomo Kenyatta.

 **Thinking & Writing**

Why did so many European countries start colonies in Africa?

_____
_____
_____
_____
_____

Unit 4, Chapter 14
Core Skills Social Studies 6, SV 9781419039058

CHAPTER 15

The Middle East

The Middle East is between three continents. Europe, Asia, and Africa all come together at the eastern end of the Mediterranean Sea. Saudi Arabia is the largest country in the Middle East.

The ancient Arabs were **nomads**. Nomads are people who move from place to place in search of food and water. Some Arabs are still nomads today. However, most people in the Middle East today live in towns and cities. In this chapter, you will read about what the Middle East was like over a thousand years ago. You will also read about what it is like to live there today.

➤ **Look at the map below. Name four countries in the Middle East besides Saudi Arabia.**

_____

Use the distance scale on the map. What is the approximate distance in miles between Cairo and Jerusalem?

_____

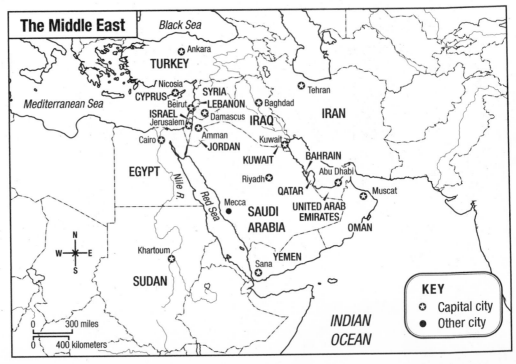

A New Religion

Most people who live in the Middle East today follow a religion called **Islam**. You remember that both Judaism and Christianity began in the Middle East. Islam also began there. The people who follow Islam are called Muslims. Like Jews and Christians, Muslims believe in one god.

Islam was founded by a religious leader named Muhammad, who lived in Mecca in the early 600s. One day Muhammad was praying in a mountain cave. He heard a voice tell him that there was only one god, named Allah. The voice said that Muhammad was the messenger of Allah. About 610, Muhammad began to teach people in the city of Mecca about Allah. Soon Muhammad had many followers. His religion was now called Islam. *Islam* means "surrender to God."

➤ **Look at the map on page 102. In what country is the city of Mecca located?**

_____

Near what body of water is Mecca located?

_____

The Spread of Islam

Muhammad died in 632. Other Muslim leaders continued to spread Islam throughout the Middle East. Muslim armies conquered people and taught them to believe in Islam. By the 800s, the Muslims had created a huge empire in the Middle East. It lasted for hundreds of years.

Islam is still a major religion. Today, millions of Muslims follow the teachings of the Koran, the holy book of Islam. The Koran teaches that every Muslim has certain duties to Islam. Muslims believe that five religious duties are so important that they are part of their everyday life. They call these duties the Five Pillars of Islam. Let's look at them more closely.

The Five Pillars of Islam

The duty of **faith** is very important to Islam. This means that all Muslims must state that they believe in one god and in Muhammad as the person who speaks for god. The duty of **prayer** means that Muslims must pray five times every day. Muslims always turn toward Mecca to pray because this is where Muhammad first began to teach.

The third Muslim duty, or Pillar of Islam, is giving help to the poor. Muslims must give money, or **alms**, to the poor.

Fasting and a **pilgrimage** are the fourth and fifth Pillars of Islam. *Fasting* means "to go without eating." The ninth month on the Muslim calendar is called Ramadan. During Ramadan, Muslims are not supposed to eat or drink between dawn and sunset. A pilgrimage is a trip made for religious reasons. Muslims are expected to travel to Mecca at least once in their lives.

The Arts

The Koran has other religious rules that have shaped the culture of the Middle East. For example, the Koran discourages artists from painting or making a sculpture of living creatures, especially human beings. As a result, some of the greatest artistic achievements in the Middle East have been in architecture and poetry.

Islamic design

Muslims praying

A Muslim woman wears a long black chador in public.

The Family

Family duties are also very important in Islamic countries. Most people live together as an **extended family**. An extended family may include a child's parents, grandparents, aunts, uncles, and cousins. According to Islamic law, a man may have as many as four wives. But a woman may have only one husband.

In some countries, men and women are separated in most areas of life. They often do not meet outside the family. Women in many Islamic cultures wear an all-covering black robe, called a *chador*, in public. Sometimes a veil is also worn so that only the eyes can be seen. Many Muslims who follow the Koran believe that no men outside a woman's family should see her unless she is wearing a chador.

The father is head of an Islamic family. He has to provide food and shelter. In return, the family is expected to obey him.

➤ **Why is the Muslim woman in the photograph wearing a chador?**

_____

_____

Oil in the Middle East

Oil is also known as **petroleum**. For hundreds of years, people knew there was oil in the Middle East. Yet they did not have much use for it. Then people began using oil as an important energy resource. Oil was used to run factories. Oil is also used to make gasoline for cars.

The Oil Boom

What does oil mean to the countries of the Middle East? It means that someone who once worked as a farmer might now work in the oil business. Many people who were once poor have become rich. It also means that the son of a shopkeeper might go to college. Most of the world's oil is located in the Middle East. Money from the sale of oil has made many countries in the Middle East rich.

Oil is the main resource in the Middle East. But once oil is used up, it cannot be renewed. Many countries could lose their wealth if the oil is used up.

In 1960, a group of oil-producing nations joined together. This group calls itself OPEC (Organization of Petroleum Exporting Countries). OPEC controls much of the oil sold around the world. OPEC decides how much oil will cost. OPEC also controls how much oil is brought out of the earth.

➤ **Look at the graph below. How much oil and gas did Saudi Arabia produce per day in 2006?**

_____

What does the graph tell you about oil production in the United States?

_____

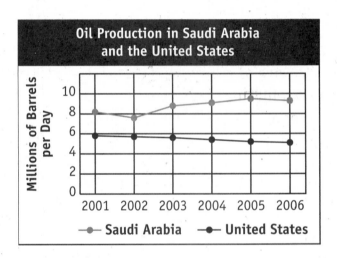

Oil Production in Saudi Arabia and the United States

Oil is a very valuable resource. In 1990, Iraq, under Saddam Hussein, attacked the oil fields of Kuwait. The United States led an international army in the Persian Gulf War. The army fought to protect the oil fields of Kuwait. Iraq was defeated, and oil continued to flow in the region.

Chapter Checkup ✓

➤ **Darken the circle by the answer that best completes each sentence.**

1. Muhammad began to teach people in Mecca that
   Ⓐ they should pray to many gods.
   Ⓑ they should leave Saudi Arabia.
   Ⓒ all Arabs should live as nomads.
   Ⓓ there is only one god.

2. Today, most people in the Middle East are followers of
   Ⓐ Christianity.
   Ⓑ Islam.
   Ⓒ polytheism.
   Ⓓ Judaism.

3. The Five Pillars of Islam are faith, prayer, alms, fasting, and
   Ⓐ pilgrimage.
   Ⓑ hope.
   Ⓒ peace.
   Ⓓ laws.

4. Many Arab families live together
   Ⓐ to practice Judaism.
   Ⓑ in houses with pillars.
   Ⓒ as an extended family.
   Ⓓ and wear orange robes in public.

5. An important resource in the Middle East is
   Ⓐ OPEC.
   Ⓑ lumber.
   Ⓒ petroleum.
   Ⓓ poetry.

6. The discovery of oil in the Middle East
   Ⓐ has not changed the way people live.
   Ⓑ has made many countries rich.
   Ⓒ has made many Arabs poor.
   Ⓓ was not as important as the discovery of petroleum.

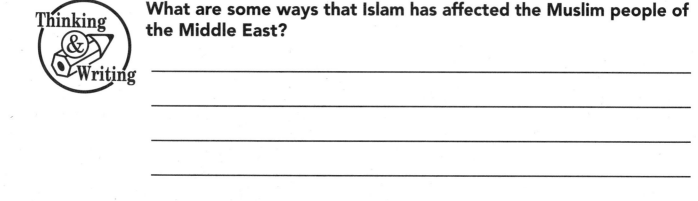

What are some ways that Islam has affected the Muslim people of the Middle East?

_____

_____

_____

_____

_____

_____

Asia

Asia is the largest continent on Earth. It has many different kinds of land regions and climates. In fact, almost every kind of land region on Earth can be found in Asia. The highest place on Earth—Mount Everest—can be found in Asia. Asia also has some of the world's largest deserts, highest plateaus, and thickest rain forests.

More than half of the world's people live in Asia. They live in more than 40 different independent nations. In this chapter, we will take a closer look at India, China, and Japan, three of the largest countries in Asia. We will also look at Korea, Taiwan, Hong Kong, and Singapore.

India

In Chapter 6, you learned about the early civilization of India. During the Middle Ages, Europeans learned about India's many resources. In time, European traders traveled to India.

By 1660, England had become a major sea and trading power. India's power was growing weaker. The rulers of India were fighting among themselves. The British were able to take over many Indian ports when they arrived in India. In the 1800s, the British made India a colony of Great Britain.

The British in India

Under British rule, life changed in India. The British built schools and factories. They also improved transportation by building railroads. All these changes helped India become more modern. The British also forced their language and way of life on India. They encouraged poor Indians to leave their farms and move to the cities to work in factories.

➤ **Why do you think the British wanted to make India a colony?**

_____

_____

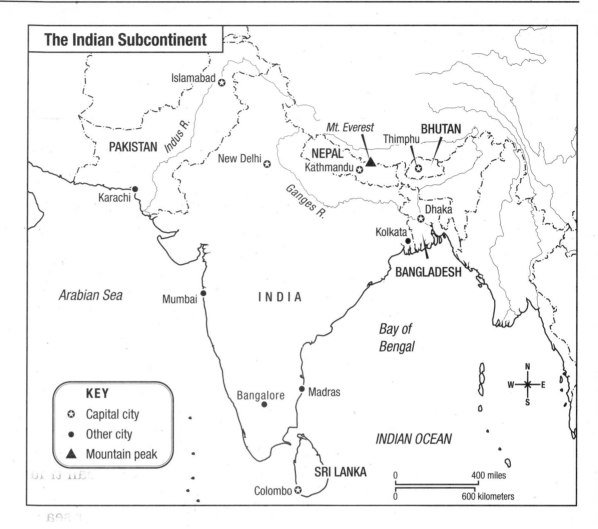

The Indian Subcontinent

India and Pakistan

Throughout the early 1900s, groups of Indians used force to drive out the British. The Indians attacked British offices and factories. But one Indian leader had a different idea. His name was Mohandas Gandhi. He called on his followers to use **nonviolent**, or peaceful, ways to drive out the British. He also called for **civil disobedience**—breaking unfair laws as a way to protest them. By the end of World War II, in 1945, the British offered India its independence.

Still, India's troubles were not over. At that time, the nation was divided between Muslims and Hindus. India's Muslims were afraid that the Hindus would control the new nation. In 1947, Indian and British leaders decided it would be best to divide India into two nations. Those nations were India and Pakistan. Most Muslims moved to Pakistan. Most Hindus remained in India.

➤ **Look at the map on this page. Circle the capital of Pakistan. Underline the capital of India.**

Indira Gandhi

India Today

One of Gandhi's followers, Jawaharlal Nehru, became India's first prime minister in 1947. Gandhi and Nehru had two different dreams for India. Gandhi dreamed of returning India to its old ways of life. "Go to the villages," he said. "That is India, there lies the soul of India." Gandhi thought the nation would be strongest if the people lived in villages and ran small businesses and farms for a living. But Nehru wanted India to become a great industrial power.

Nehru's dream came true. Today, India is one of Asia's most important industrial nations. It has many modern factories. These factories make many products, such as iron goods, cars, and textiles. India has a very good educational system. Indian students are among the best trained in the world in science and technology. Science and technology have become an important part of the economy.

Yet India is also a nation of villagers. Most of India's huge population lives in villages. The people live much as they always have, although many now use tractors instead of animals to plow their fields.

Nehru's daughter, Indira Gandhi, served as prime minister from 1966 to 1977 and from 1980 to 1984. She was the first woman prime minister of India. She was murdered in office. Her son Rajiv Gandhi was prime minister from 1984 to 1989. During the 1991 elections, Rajiv Gandhi was murdered. In 1998, Atal Behari Vajpayee became India's prime minister. He was replaced by Manmohan Singh Kohli in 2004.

Religious and political violence continued to be problems. In the late 1980s, Muslim groups in Kashmir, a region of India, protested Indian rule. These protests became violent. Both India and Pakistan claim parts of Kashmir, and the countries have fought over the issue. In 2004, India and Pakistan again began peace talks.

Population growth is a serious concern in India. By the year 2000, India's population was larger than one billion people. Indians are working hard to find ways to feed and house their growing population.

➤ **What is the main problem that India faces today?**

China

In the early 1270s, a young Italian, Marco Polo, traveled to Asia with his father and uncle. When he returned to Italy over 20 years later, he amazed people with the tales of his travels in China. He told of big cities filled with beautiful buildings and parks.

Remember that in ancient times, China was ruled by families called dynasties. In 1644, warriors from the plains of Manchuria pushed out the ruling family. The Manchu warriors started a new dynasty that lasted until 1912!

➤ **Look at the map below. Put an X on Manchuria.**

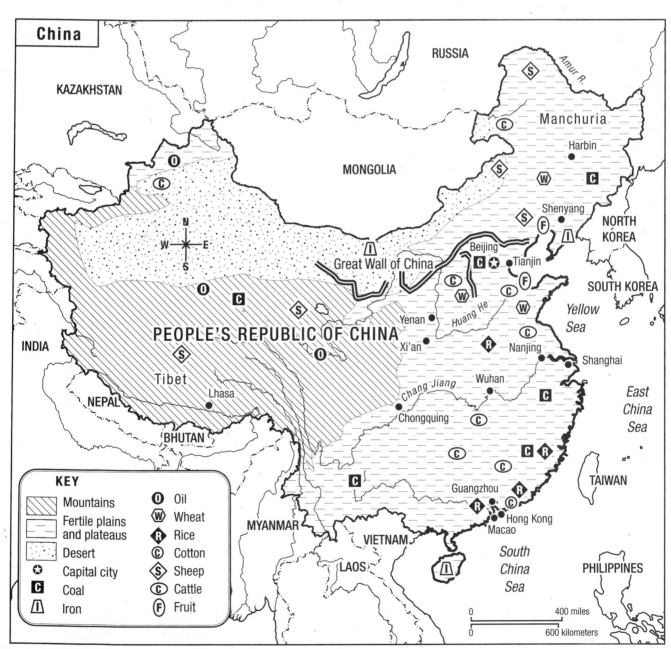

Europeans Arrive in China

Marco Polo's stories made many Europeans interested in Asia. European traders began looking for easier routes to China. The Portuguese arrived in China in 1514. The coming of the Europeans led to a long period of unrest in China. China's emperors did not trust the European traders. They were not interested in buying European goods.

In the 1700s, the Manchu emperors would let European traders into only a few of their ports. But the Europeans did not give up. There was too much money to be made buying and selling Chinese goods, especially tea. The British began to look for a product that they could sell in China.

In time, the British found that product. It was **opium**, a very dangerous drug. This made China's rulers very angry. They worried that China would become poor if the Chinese spent all their money on opium. War started in 1839 between the Chinese and the British. But the Chinese were unable to make the British leave China. The Chinese lost the war in 1842. They signed a treaty with the Europeans. The treaty allowed the Europeans to trade freely in China.

Meanwhile, many Chinese people were becoming unhappy with their government. The Manchu rulers of the 1800s were not good leaders. They taxed the poor and spent the people's money on themselves.

Other countries saw that China was growing weaker. In 1894, Japan invaded China. The Japanese took over the island of Formosa, now called Taiwan, and other lands. Meanwhile, the British continued to try to control the Chinese economy. China's rulers knew that changes needed to be made, but they were unable to act quickly enough.

➤ **Look at the map on page 119. About how many miles is Japan from the island of Taiwan?**

A painting of Mao Zedong

Civil War in China

In the early 1900s, groups of **rebels** formed to save China. A rebel is someone who is not happy with the way things are and wants to change them. In 1912, rebels took over the government. This ended over 3,000 years of rule by emperors.

In 1922, the rebels divided into two main groups. The Nationalists wanted to make China a democracy. The Communists wanted a communist government like the one in the Soviet Union. In 1934, the Nationalist Army nearly destroyed the communist forces in southeast China. Only 8,000 Communists got away. They escaped to China's mountains some 6,000 miles away. Their escape became known as the Long March.

World War II ended the struggle between the Nationalists and the Communists. Both sides joined together to drive out the Japanese, who had invaded China again in 1937. But after the war, the struggle began again. This time the Communists began to win their fight with the Nationalists. Finally, in 1949, four years after World War II ended, the Communists won. Mao Zedong, the communist general, took control of China.

➤ **In what year did rule by emperors end in China? In what year did the Communists take control?**

China Under Communism

Mao had great dreams for China. He wanted to make China more modern. He also wanted to create a culture in which there would be no **poverty**. This means that China would not have any poor people. But when Mao took over the government, China had very little industry. It had very poor farms. Many people did not have enough to eat. So Mao began **reforms**, or changes, to try to make things better. He gave land to people. He built factories throughout the countryside. He also built new roads and dams.

In the mid-1950s, Mao started a program called the Great Leap Forward. Land was taken away from the people. All the farms in an area were joined together in a single unit, called a **commune**. Everyone had to work together on the communes and share their property. People who did not like Mao's changes were sometimes put in jail. In 1976, after Mao died, China's new leaders did not force people to live in communes. They allowed people to own small pieces of land.

China Today

In the spring of 1989, some Chinese students wanted more than the right to own land. They wanted democracy. They held a protest march in Tiananmen Square in the center of Beijing, China's capital. The communist leaders demanded that the protesters go home. When they refused, the government sent in the army. About 2,000 students and other protesters were killed.

The leaders of China who followed Mao Zedong wanted to control the political system even as they allowed more economic freedom. Today, some Chinese people can own private businesses. But they are not allowed to vote in free elections. China has the largest Communist Party in the world. There are some signs that China might someday become more democratic. Its economy is growing and provides a huge market for western goods.

➤ **What freedoms do people in China have today?**

_____

_____

Tiananmen Square in Beijing

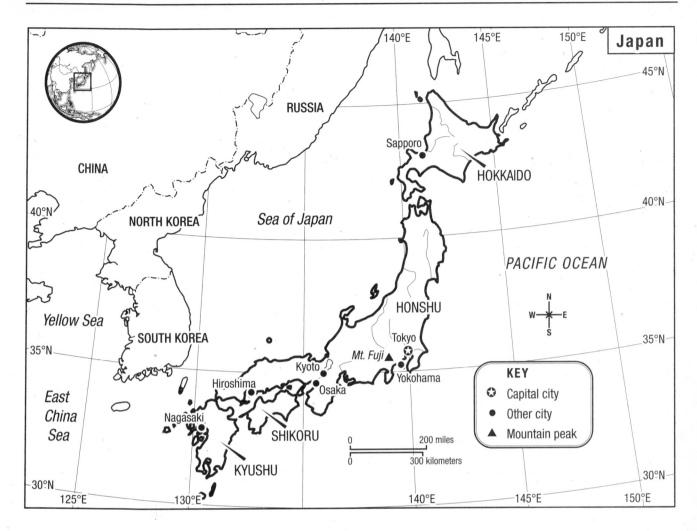

Japan

The nation of Japan lies 500 miles east of China. Look at the map above. Japan is a group of large islands. A group of islands like this is called an **archipelago**.

➤ **How many large islands make up the Japanese archipelago?**

_____

The islands of Japan are full of mountains and hills, separated by narrow valleys. Very little of the land in Japan is flat. Most of the flat land lies in the valleys and along the coast. Japan's population of more than 127 million is crowded onto this flat land.

➤ **Look again at the map. On what meridian, or line of longitude, does Tokyo lie?**

A Japanese temple

Japanese Culture

The people who lived in Japan over a thousand years ago did not trade often with people from other lands. So the Japanese had their own special culture. They lived in small family groups called **clans** and hunted, fished, and farmed for a living.

Then, beginning in the 400s, the Japanese started to trade with the Chinese. The Japanese borrowed many Chinese ideas. They copied ancient Chinese buildings and art. They also borrowed the Chinese system of writing. And like the Chinese, the Japanese were ruled by emperors.

➤ **Look at the map on page 115. Circle the name of the sea that separates Japan from North Korea.**

Japan and the West

Over time, however, Japanese culture began to change. For instance, the Japanese made their own alphabet, using Chinese characters. They worked very hard to keep their own culture. For hundreds of years, they did not trade with other countries.

Then, in 1853, four ships from the United States sailed into the harbor of Tokyo, the capital of Japan. The ships were under the command of a man named Matthew Perry. He had come to ask the Japanese to trade with the United States.

The Japanese were amazed by the U.S. steamships. They felt they had to trade with Perry. And just as Japan had once borrowed ideas from China, the Japanese soon borrowed new ideas from the United States. In less than 20 years, factories were being built in Japan. The country was on its way to becoming an important industrial nation.

Japan needed resources like oil and coal to run its factories. But Japan has few of these resources. So the Japanese began to look for other countries in Asia where they could get these resources.

By World War II, Japan had built an empire. Earlier it had taken over parts of Southeast Asia, China, and many islands in the Pacific. But Japan lost the war in 1945. Not only did Japan lose all the territory it had captured, but the country itself was nearly destroyed.

Japan's people worked hard after the war. With help from the United States, they rebuilt their cities and factories. They also started trading again. By the 1970s, Japan had become one of the world's most important industrial nations. The Japanese bought resources from other countries and turned them into goods such as cars, televisions, and cameras. Many people said Japan was an "economic miracle."

➤ **Explain why many people felt Japan was an "economic miracle."**

_____

_____

Tokyo, Japan

Japan Today

Today, Japan is one of the world's most powerful economies. It leads the world in banking and shipbuilding. Companies in Japan produce countless products, from cameras to cars. Only the United States makes more factory goods than Japan.

Life in Japan today is much the same as in the United States. People wear the same type of clothing and live in similar houses. Yet the Japanese still value their old culture. The family is still very important in Japan.

India, China, and Japan are just three nations in Asia, and there are about 40 others. But all three are very important nations, and all three are very different from one another. Like millions of other people in Asia, the people of India, China, and Japan all work to make their lives better.

➤ **Look at the circle graphs on this page. As you know, each part of the graph is a percentage of the whole. In 1997, what percentage of the U.S.–Japanese trade was imports from the United States?**

_____

Did trade between the United States and Japan increase or decrease between 1997 and 2006?

_____

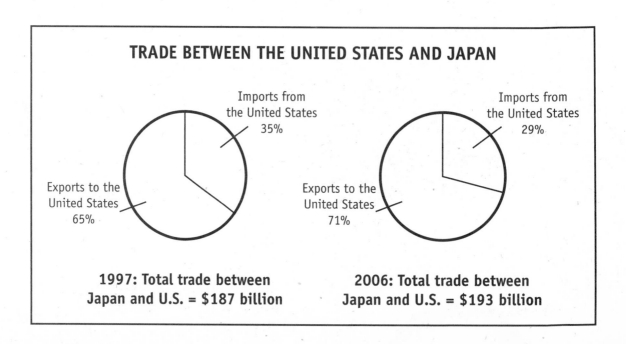

TRADE BETWEEN THE UNITED STATES AND JAPAN

Imports from the United States 35%

Exports to the United States 65%

1997: Total trade between Japan and U.S. = $187 billion

Imports from the United States 29%

Exports to the United States 71%

2006: Total trade between Japan and U.S. = $193 billion

East Asia's "Tigers"

In the 1980s, several small countries in East Asia had economies that were so successful that they were called "little tigers." Those countries were Hong Kong, South Korea, Singapore, and Taiwan.

Taiwan is a large island off the coast of China. South Korea is the southern part of the Korean peninsula in Asia. The economies of both countries depended mainly on farming in the 1950s. As both countries sold their farm products to other countries after World War II, their economies grew. Both countries also began to make products in factories to sell to other countries.

Singapore is an island nation. Hong Kong was protected by Great Britain until 1997, but since then it has been part of China. The economies of Singapore and Hong Kong developed through trade with other countries. They built factories that made products to sell to other countries. Each also became an important banking center in Asia. Today, Hong Kong is helping to fuel economic growth in China.

Together, Hong Kong, Singapore, Taiwan, and South Korea were once called the "four little tigers" of East Asia. They are still very powerful economies.

➤ **How are the "four little tigers" alike?**

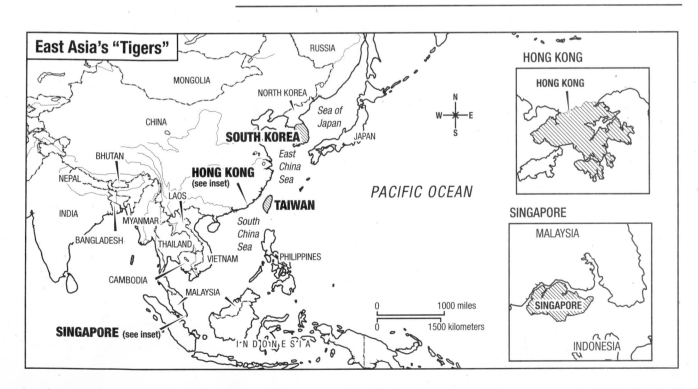

Chapter Checkup ✓

➤ **Darken the circle by the answer that best completes each sentence.**

1. In the 1800s, India became a colony of
   Ⓐ France.
   Ⓑ Great Britain.
   Ⓒ China.
   Ⓓ Pakistan.

2. Mohandas Gandhi helped India win independence through
   Ⓐ fighting.
   Ⓑ communism.
   Ⓒ nonviolent protests.
   Ⓓ industrialization.

3. War started between the Chinese and the British because
   Ⓐ the British began to sell opium in China.
   Ⓑ the British wanted to make the Chinese into slaves.
   Ⓒ the British would not buy Chinese goods.
   Ⓓ the British wanted to borrow Chinese ideas about art.

4. Mao Zedong wanted to make China
   Ⓐ a democracy.
   Ⓑ a communist nation.
   Ⓒ a colony of Great Britain.
   Ⓓ very poor.

5. The Japanese people have borrowed many ideas from
   Ⓐ Great Britain.
   Ⓑ Russia.
   Ⓒ China and the United States.
   Ⓓ India.

6. After the Japanese began to trade with the United States in the 1800s, Japan
   Ⓐ did not want to trade with other countries.
   Ⓑ fought a war with Great Britain.
   Ⓒ made its own alphabet, using Chinese characters.
   Ⓓ became an important industrial nation.

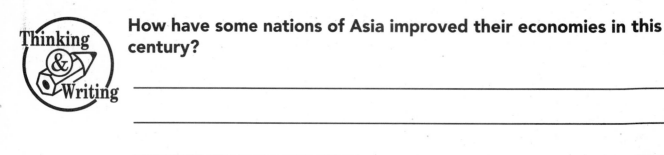

How have some nations of Asia improved their economies in this century?

_____

_____

_____

_____

_____

_____

CHAPTER 17
Oceania

The Pacific Ocean is the largest ocean in the world. In the southern Pacific, there are many thousands of islands. Some of these islands are too small even to appear on a map. The island of Australia, however, is large enough to be a continent.

In this chapter, you will read more about Australia and another island nation in the South Pacific called New Zealand. We call this part of the world Oceania.

➤ **The picture on this page shows the harbor of Sydney, a major city in Australia. Does Sydney look like an old city or a modern new city?**

The Pacific Islands

The thousands of islands in Oceania are divided into three groups. They are called Polynesia, Micronesia, and Melanesia. Our state of Hawaii is made up of several islands in Polynesia.

The islands in the South Pacific were formed by volcanoes thousands of years ago. Most of the islands are actually the tops of huge mountains under the sea!

New Zealand

The country of New Zealand is made up of several dozen small islands and two main islands. The main islands are called North Island and South Island. The climate in New Zealand is mild because the country is surrounded by the ocean.

Sydney Harbor and the Sydney Opera House

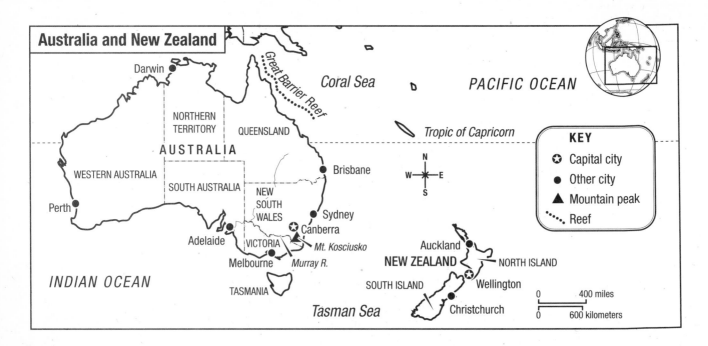

The "Land Down Under"

The name *Australia* means "southern land." The entire continent lies south of the equator. Although Australia is surrounded by water, it is a very dry continent. About one third of the land is desert. Australia's hot, dry plains are known as the **outback**.

➤ **Look at the map on this page. What are the capital cities of Australia and New Zealand?**

_____

Look at the time zone map on page 9. When it's 10 P.M. in Sydney, what time is it in London?

_____

The Aborigines of Australia

The first people who lived in Australia probably came from islands in the South Pacific about 40,000 years ago. These early people are known today as **Aborigines**. The word *aborigine* means "the first known people to live in a place." The Aborigines hunted and gathered their food. They did not farm or build villages. They traveled throughout Australia in groups of a few families.

Boomerang

In order to live in the deserts of Australia, the Aborigines needed special tools. They used stone axes, spears, and a weapon for hunting known as a **boomerang**. Boomerangs are curved, flat pieces of wood or animal bone. When thrown in the air, boomerangs will often return to the thrower. The Aborigines discovered that water collected in the roots of large bushes. They used digging sticks to dig roots out of the ground. They learned to use knowledge and skill to stay alive in the Australian desert.

The Maori of New Zealand

The first people to live in New Zealand were known as the **Maori**. They probably came to New Zealand from Polynesia. They sailed great distances over the sea in large canoes. Like the Aborigines of Australia, the Maori continue to live in New Zealand today.

Like the Aborigines, the Maori were hunters. However, the Maori also grew some crops. They grew sweet potatoes and beans on their farms. And instead of moving from place to place, the Maori built houses of reeds.

Statues of Maori gods

Europeans Discover Oceania

The first Europeans to come to Oceania were Dutch explorers and traders. In 1606, a Dutch explorer named Willem Jansz landed in northern Australia. He was followed in 1642 by another Dutch explorer, Abel Tasman. Tasman landed on an island near Australia. This island was later named Tasmania, after Abel Tasman.

Captain James Cook

Tasman also reached New Zealand and named it after a part of the Netherlands called Zealand. But Tasman did not stay long in Oceania. He thought that Australia and New Zealand were not important because the people there did not have what he considered valuable goods to trade.

➤ **Look at the map on page 122. Circle two areas named after Abel Tasman.**

In 1769, about 100 years after Tasman's journey, a British explorer named Captain James Cook landed in New Zealand. On the same voyage, he also explored Australia. Cook realized that both places had good land for farming. He thought they would be good places for settlers.

Australia and New Zealand Become Nations

The first British settlers to come to Australia were **convicts**. Convicts are people who are found guilty of breaking the law. Great Britain sent the first convicts to Australia in 1788. They had to work there as punishment for their crimes. Over the next two centuries, however, many settlers who were not convicts also came to Australia.

In 1851, gold was discovered in Australia. Then more people moved to the country. By 1860, colonies had been created in eastern Australia and on the west coast. Australia continued to be ruled by Great Britain until 1901. Then Australians united to become the Commonwealth of Australia.

The first Europeans to go to New Zealand were traders and hunters. They went during the 1700s to trade with the Maori and to hunt seals and whales near the islands. During the early 1800s, British traders and hunters began settling in New Zealand.

New Zealand did not become a British colony until 1840. In that year a British officer named William Hobson signed a peace treaty with the Maori. This treaty gave Great Britain control over New Zealand.

Even though the Maori had signed the treaty, they were unhappy. They did not want to be forced to sell their land to the British. And more British kept coming to New Zealand. Finally, in 1845 the Maori began to fight the British for control of New Zealand. The fighting continued off and on until 1872, when the Maori surrendered.

Queen Charlotte Sound, New Zealand

By 1900, the colonists of New Zealand felt that Great Britain should let them govern New Zealand themselves. Great Britain agreed. In 1907, New Zealand became a nation with its own elected government.

Life in Oceania Today

Today, Australia is one of the richest countries in the world. This is because Australia has many natural resources. These resources have helped Australia become a modern industrial nation. Australian cities are much like American cities.

Fishing and farming are still important in New Zealand and the other, smaller Pacific islands. In large cities in New Zealand and some other Pacific islands, people work in offices or stores. But people on some of the smallest Pacific islands still live much the way people have lived there for centuries. They fish and plant crops for food. Sometimes they buy other goods from ships that cross the Pacific. They also sell food products, such as coconuts and potatoes, all over the world.

Modern-day Aborigines in Australia and Maori in New Zealand play an increasing role in their societies. They are adapting to the modern world. Some work in cities and have jobs in technology. Others still live and work in rural areas.

➤ **When did New Zealand become a nation?**

Chapter Checkup ✓

➤ **Darken the circle by the answer that best completes each sentence.**

1. Oceania includes Australia, New Zealand, and
   - Ⓐ the outback.
   - Ⓑ the Southern Alps.
   - Ⓒ more than 10,000 islands in the South Pacific.
   - Ⓓ more than 10,000 islands in the Atlantic Ocean.

2. The Aborigines
   - Ⓐ farmed and built villages.
   - Ⓑ built large cities.
   - Ⓒ came to Australia after the British arrived there.
   - Ⓓ hunted and gathered their food.

3. The Maori grew crops and built houses out of reeds in
   - Ⓐ Australia.
   - Ⓑ New Zealand.
   - Ⓒ Polynesia.
   - Ⓓ Melanesia.

4. The first British settlers to come to Australia were
   - Ⓐ convicts.
   - Ⓑ farmers.
   - Ⓒ government workers.
   - Ⓓ hunters.

5. More people began settling in Australia after 1851 because
   - Ⓐ it was a good place to farm.
   - Ⓑ they wanted to trade with New Zealand.
   - Ⓒ they had broken the law.
   - Ⓓ gold was discovered there.

6. The Maori began to fight the British for control of New Zealand because
   - Ⓐ they did not want to be forced to sell their land to the British.
   - Ⓑ they did not want to live in cities.
   - Ⓒ they wanted to live on only one of New Zealand's islands.
   - Ⓓ they wanted to work in offices and stores.

Thinking & Writing

Compare and contrast how life was different for the Maori of New Zealand and the Aborigines of Australia.

_____

_____

_____

_____

_____

Name _____   Date _____

| Unit 4 | Skill Builder | Reading a Double Line Graph |

Remember that more than half of the world's population lives in Asia. India and China both have very large populations. Use the line graph below to compare the population figures for both countries from the years 1960 to 2000.

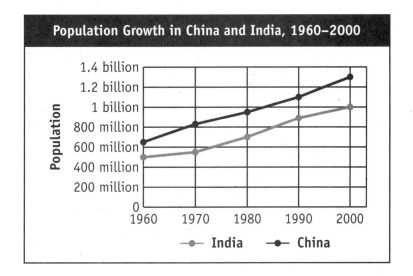

1. According to the graph, did India ever have a larger population than China?

_____

2. What was the population of India in 1990?

_____

3. In what year did the population of China pass one billion?

_____

4. In this unit, you read that India's population became larger than one billion people by the year 2000. Do you think India's population will be above 1.5 billion by 2010? Use the information from the graph to explain your answer.

_____

_____

_____

_____

Unit 4  Test

➤ **Darken the circle by the answer that best completes each sentence.**

1. Much of North Africa is covered by
   (A) monsoons.
   (B) desert.
   (C) forests.
   (D) mountains.

2. The dictator who led the Soviet Union during the early years of the Cold War was
   (A) Joseph Stalin.
   (B) Lech Walesa.
   (C) Mikhail Gorbachev.
   (D) Boris Yeltsin.

3. In 1945, diplomats met in San Francisco to form
   (A) Solidarity.
   (B) the prime meridian.
   (C) the Communist Party.
   (D) the United Nations.

4. Most people in the Middle East today follow a religion called
   (A) Christianity.
   (B) Judaism.
   (C) Islam.
   (D) Hinduism.

5. Nonviolence and civil disobedience were urged by
   (A) Mao Zedong.
   (B) Mohandas Gandhi.
   (C) Marco Polo.
   (D) James Cook.

6. The first people to live in New Zealand were the
   (A) Maori.
   (B) Aborigines.
   (C) convicts.
   (D) Dutch explorers.

Thinking & Writing

Do you think glasnost contributed to the end of communism in the Soviet Union? Why or why not?

_____

_____

_____

_____

_____

_____

_____

CHAPTER 18 The Western Hemisphere: Geography and Climate

Earth has seven continents. Four are in the Eastern Hemisphere: Asia, Africa, Australia, and Europe. Antarctica is in both hemispheres. Only two continents are in the Western Hemisphere: North and South America. In this chapter, you will learn more about what these two continents are like.

The Americas

In 1507, the name *America* was first used on a map of South America. The mapmaker used information from an Italian explorer named Amerigo Vespucci. Since this land had no name, the mapmaker decided to name it after the explorer, Amerigo Vespucci.

Early Explorers

Christopher Columbus did not reach South America until his third trip in 1498. By that time, other explorers had started to cross the Atlantic Ocean. In 1496, King Henry VII of England asked an Italian sailor named John Cabot to sail to America. In early May 1497, Cabot sailed with 18 men on a small ship called *Matthew*. Cabot landed on the east coast of Canada on June 24, 1497. He did not find the gold he had hoped for. But he did find rivers filled with fish and huge forests full of tall pine trees.

➤ **What ocean did Cabot sail across to reach Canada?**

_____

What do you think it might have been like to travel with Cabot and his men? Today, the Western Hemisphere has many busy cities. But you can still travel through North and South America and see the same rivers and land regions the first explorers saw.

129

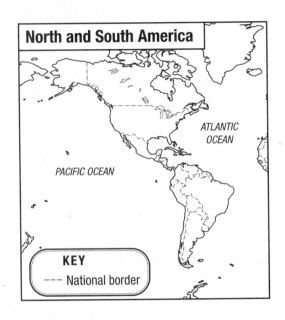

North and South America

ATLANTIC OCEAN

PACIFIC OCEAN

KEY
--- National border

Canada

It's a good thing that John Cabot did not sail to Canada in the fall. The climate in Canada is very cold because it is so far north. In fact, parts of northern Canada are covered with snow and ice all year round.

In the winter, the west coast of Canada is the warmest part of the country. Ocean currents move up from the South Pacific. These currents carry warm water. The currents warm the air, and the air warms the west coast.

Southeastern Canada has cold winters and short summers. More than half of the people of Canada live in the southeast. Two of Canada's biggest cities, Montreal and Toronto, are found here. The St. Lawrence River and the five Great Lakes form the lower border of this area.

➤ **Is the west coast of Canada warmer or colder than the east coast?**

Alberta, Canada

The largest part of Canada is the **Canadian Shield**. This is a flat region that borders Hudson Bay. There are thousands of beautiful lakes in the Canadian Shield. The land and the weather are not good for farming, but resources such as gold and lumber can be found here.

West of Hudson Bay lie Canada's flat Interior Plains. Huge farms are found in the southern part of the plains. Large forests cover the northern part. West of the plains are the tall Rocky Mountains and, finally, the Pacific Ocean. Long ago, glaciers carved valleys between the mountains. These valleys became long, narrow bays called **fjords**.

The United States

The United States and Canada have many of the same land regions. In the east, the Appalachian Mountains go from Canada almost to the Gulf of Mexico. In the west, the Rocky Mountains go from Canada through the United States and into Mexico. The Great Plains of the United States are part of the same land region as Canada's Interior Plains. But the climate in the Great Plains is not as cold as the plains region in Canada.

Our most northern state, Alaska, has places that are so cold the sun never melts the snow! Alaska's climate and land regions are much the same as Canada's colder regions. There are even fjords along the coast. The United States does have climates and land regions that Canada does not have. The islands of Hawaii, in the Pacific Ocean, have a tropical climate. The weather there never gets cold.

There are also deserts in the United States. One desert in California gets so hot that it is called Death Valley! It is the hottest region in the United States. Deserts cover large parts of several states in the Southwest. But deserts in the United States are much smaller than the deserts of North Africa, Asia, and Australia.

➤ **What are two kinds of land regions that the United States and Canada have in common?**

The Grand Canyon is a popular U.S. destination.

Mexico and Central America

There are more than a dozen other countries on or near the continent of North America. Some are islands in the Caribbean Sea. Others, including Mexico, are on the land that curves south of the United States. We call the countries south of Mexico Central America.

Mexico and the countries of Central America have warm climates. Large areas of thick rain forests make the land difficult to farm.

Panama is a country in Central America. It is a very narrow country. That is why Panama was chosen as a place to dig a **canal** to connect the Atlantic Ocean and the Pacific Ocean. A canal is a waterway, like a river, that is built across land.

➤ **Find Panama on the map on page 143. What route did ships traveling from the Atlantic Ocean to the Pacific Ocean have to take before the Panama Canal was built?**

Building the Panama Canal

The building of the Panama Canal was a great achievement. The canal is over 50 miles long. The canal is very important because it connects two oceans. Ships sailing between New York City and San Francisco can shorten their trip by almost 8,000 miles by using the canal. Without the canal, they would have to go around the tip of South America.

It took ten years to build the Panama Canal.

The builders of the canal had to solve many problems. Before the digging could begin, workers had to drain swamps and clear land. Giant swarms of mosquitoes that carried deadly sicknesses lived in these swamps. Many workers died before the problem was brought under control. The next problem involved digging through tons of rock and dirt. **Locks** also had to be built. Locks look like a set of steps. They are gated areas in a canal where ships can be raised from one level to another.

The Atlantic entrance is a 7-mile channel that connects to a series of locks that raise ships 85 feet. The ships go through a series of locks and connecting lakes. Just before reaching the Pacific, there is a two-step drop to the level of the Pacific Ocean.

Ships are towed through the canal by electric engines on tracks along the lock walls. It takes anywhere from 15 to 20 hours to pass through the Panama Canal.

➤ **Why is the Panama Canal important?**

_____

South America

If you travel south from Central America, you will reach the continent of South America. North and South America look a little bit alike. Flat plains lie in the middle of both continents. High mountains can be found on the west side of each continent, too. Places at the southern tip of South America get very cold in the winter. Countries near the equator are hot all year.

The mountains in South America are part of the same mountain range that passes through North America. In the United States and Canada, these mountains are called the Rockies. In South America, they are known as the Andes. There are many volcanoes in this mountain range.

Most of the flat land of South America is a huge, bowl-like area called the **Amazon Basin**. The Amazon River flows from the Andes through this basin to the Atlantic Ocean. Most of the Amazon Basin is covered with a tropical rain forest.

The Andes mountain range is 4,500 miles long.

➤ **Name two ways in which North and South America are alike.**

_____

_____

The Rain Forest

The Amazon rain forest is the largest and oldest rain forest in the world. The climate is very warm and wet. Because of the climate, the rain forest is always green. Trees grow very tall, and many other lush plants grow there. The Amazon rain forest covers about one third of South America.

The Amazon rain forest is home to the greatest variety of plant and animal life on Earth. An acre of forest land in the Amazon rain forest may contain more than 200 kinds of trees. There are more kinds of snakes, birds, insects, mammals, frogs, and other animals in the rain forest than anywhere else.

Many scientists believe that the plant life in the rain forest may offer medicines for some human diseases. There are many plants in the forest that have not yet been identified. These plants could provide new medicines for people.

Today, the plant and animal life in the rain forest is threatened. Human population growth is dangerous to the rain forest. People have destroyed large areas of the forest in order to clear land for farming. Other people have cut down trees for wood. The loss of large areas of the rain forest will mean that different kinds of plants and animals no longer have a place to live.

Despite efforts to save the rain forest in South America, trees are still being cut down. As the Amazon rain forest disappears, life on Earth could change. Some experts are concerned that the rain forest in Brazil could be entirely gone by 2050.

The Amazon rain forest

Chapter Checkup ✓

➤ **Darken the circle by the answer that best completes each sentence.**

1. North and South America are both in the
   Ⓐ Eastern Hemisphere.
   Ⓑ Western Hemisphere.
   Ⓒ Northern Hemisphere.
   Ⓓ Southern Hemisphere.

2. The west coast of Canada stays warmer than the east coast because
   Ⓐ it is covered with snow and ice.
   Ⓑ many people live there.
   Ⓒ it is closer to the equator.
   Ⓓ ocean currents from the South Pacific warm the air.

3. One land region the United States has that Canada does not have is
   Ⓐ deserts.
   Ⓑ rivers.
   Ⓒ mountains.
   Ⓓ plains.

4. The Panama Canal connects the Atlantic Ocean with the
   Ⓐ Canadian Shield.
   Ⓑ Hudson Bay.
   Ⓒ Pacific Ocean.
   Ⓓ Amazon River.

5. The Rocky Mountains are part of the same mountain range as the
   Ⓐ equator.
   Ⓑ Appalachian Mountains.
   Ⓒ Canadian Shield.
   Ⓓ Andes.

6. In the Amazon Basin, there is a large
   Ⓐ rain forest.
   Ⓑ mountain range.
   Ⓒ desert.
   Ⓓ hemisphere.

Thinking & Writing America is named for Amerigo Vespucci. What other names might America have been given? Think of other people who were part of the exploration of the Western Hemisphere. Make up names for America based on their names.

_____

_____

_____

_____

_____

CHAPTER 19 Canada

In the 1970s, a group of world leaders held a meeting in Canada. Before they arrived, the Canadian people decided they wanted to show the leaders as much as possible about their culture. They decided the visitors should stay at a hotel shaped like a log cabin. This would show the leaders that Canada has a pioneer past and is a land with many beautiful forests.

In this chapter, you will read more about Canada's past. You will also see how Canada changed from a huge wilderness to a modern nation. Today, Canada is the second-largest country in the world.

➤ **Why would a cabin made of logs help visitors realize that Canada has many forests?**

_____

Canada's Geography

In the last chapter, you read that Canada is a land with many tall mountains. Look at the **elevation map** on page 137. *Elevation* means "how high a place is." An elevation map shows the actual height of mountains, plateaus, plains, and other landforms. This height is usually measured in feet or meters above sea level.

Study the elevation key on the map. You can see that each pattern shows a different elevation. You can figure out the elevation of a place by its pattern on the map.

➤ **At what elevation is the town of Whitehorse? Write your answer in feet.**

_____

Ottawa, national capital of Canada

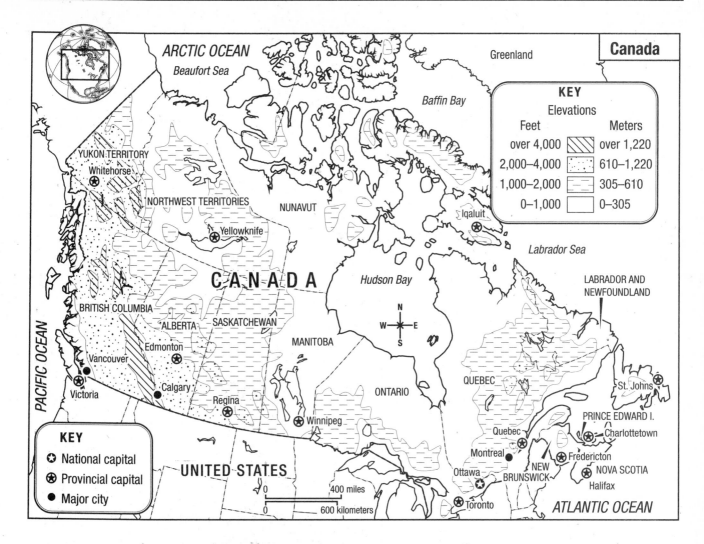

The First Europeans in Canada

    The Vikings were the first Europeans to visit Canada. They traveled across the Atlantic in small, swift sailing ships. The Vikings probably reached the region we call Newfoundland about A.D. 1000. They settled there but did not stay long.

    Five hundred years passed before another group of European explorers arrived and claimed lands in Canada. In 1497 an explorer named John Cabot claimed Newfoundland for England. He was followed by several French explorers. A Frenchman named Jacques Cartier sailed up the St. Lawrence River in 1534. Probably the most famous explorer of Canada, however, was an Englishman named Henry Hudson. He explored a huge bay in northern Canada in 1610. Later, this bay was named Hudson Bay.

➤ **Look at the map above. Circle Hudson Bay on the map.**

The First Colonies in Canada

Europeans wanted to create colonies in Canada because of the resources there. Fishing boats took huge amounts of fish back to Europe. Furs were even more valuable. French traders bought the skins of beavers and other animals from American Indians and sold them in Europe.

Settlers in Quebec, Canada, 1870s

Great Britain and France Fight Over Canada

English explorers began to settle in Canada in the early 1600s. At the same time, a French explorer named Samuel de Champlain founded the city of Quebec. Then, in 1670, English traders formed the Hudson's Bay Company. It controlled the fur trade in the huge region around Hudson Bay. It wasn't long before the French and British began to fight each other in Canada. They fought over control of land and trade.

Between 1754 and 1763, the British and French fought the French and Indian War. Each side fought with the help of different American Indian groups. Great Britain won this war in 1763 and gained control of Canada.

Canada Under British Rule

Canada remained under British control for a little over 100 years. But the British allowed the French Canadians to keep their laws, language, and religion. During the time of British rule, new inventions like the locomotive helped Canadians travel and settle in the western part of Canada.

Becoming a Nation

In 1867, Canada won the right to self-government. The Canadian people were finally able to elect their own leaders. Then, in 1871, Canada gained the land that is now known as British Columbia. Now Canada's borders reached from the Atlantic Ocean to the Pacific Ocean. At about the same time, the Canadian Pacific Railroad was completed. This railroad joined eastern Canada with British Columbia.

The flag of Canada

Modern Canada

Besides its British and French population, Canada is home to people from many other lands. Also, thousands of American Indians still make Canada their home. They were the first people to live there. All of these people bring their many different cultures to Canada.

The Canadian government recognizes the different cultures of Canada. It started a program called **multiculturalism**. *Multi* means "many" in Latin. So you can probably guess what *multiculturalism* means. The government hopes that if Canadians share their different ways of life, Canada will be a richer, stronger nation.

In the 1990s, Canada had its first woman prime minister. Kim Campbell, leader of the Progressive Conservative Party, served in that position from June 1993 until November 1993.

Quebec

Multiculturalism has created some problems for Canada, however. At times, many people who live in Quebec have wanted their province to **secede**, or leave Canada and become a separate nation.

French culture is everywhere in Quebec. Most people speak French. Many people argue that too many businesses in Quebec belong to English-speaking owners. French-speaking people, they say, do not get enough good jobs. For now, Quebec has voted to stay part of Canada.

Northern Canada

Canada's northern lands—Yukon Territory, the Northwest Territories, and Nunavut—make up more than one third of Canada's land. Because much of the land has long, cold winters and short summers, fewer than 100,000 people live in these areas. But Nunavut, Yukon, and the Northwest Territories are rich in oil and minerals such as gold and silver. Most people in the north have mining or oil-company jobs.

➤ **What does this picture tell you about life in the northern parts of Canada?**

_____

_____

Chapter Checkup ✔

➤ **Darken the circle by the answer that best completes each sentence.**

1. Canada is
   - Ⓐ one of the largest countries in the world.
   - Ⓑ the smallest country in the world.
   - Ⓒ the smallest country in North America.
   - Ⓓ much smaller than the United States.

2. An elevation map shows
   - Ⓐ the distances between major cities.
   - Ⓑ the populations of cities and nations.
   - Ⓒ the cities that have the most elevators.
   - Ⓓ the height of different land regions.

3. The first people to live in Canada were
   - Ⓐ French explorers.
   - Ⓑ English explorers.
   - Ⓒ American Indians.
   - Ⓓ Spanish explorers.

4. Hudson Bay in Canada was named after
   - Ⓐ Jacques Cartier.
   - Ⓑ Henry Hudson.
   - Ⓒ Christopher Columbus.
   - Ⓓ John Cabot.

5. The British and French fought each other in Canada because
   - Ⓐ they both wanted to build a railroad across Canada.
   - Ⓑ they wanted to control Canadian land and trade.
   - Ⓒ they both wanted to settle the city of Quebec.
   - Ⓓ French Canadians wanted to use British laws.

6. At times, many people of Quebec have wanted their province to
   - Ⓐ become part of the United States.
   - Ⓑ become a colony of France.
   - Ⓒ become the capital of Canada.
   - Ⓓ secede from the rest of Canada.

List and describe some of the different cultures that make up Canada.

_____

_____

_____

_____

_____

_____

CHAPTER 20 Latin America

Do you remember reading about the Maya, Aztecs, and Inca? These American Indians lived in Latin America thousands of years ago. Latin America is another name for Mexico, Central America, and South America.

People from Europe arrived in Latin America about 500 years ago. The first European people to arrive were from Spain and Portugal. Later, slaves were brought from Africa to work on plantations. In this chapter, you will read what happened after the Europeans arrived in Latin America and what life is like there today.

➤ **Look at the map on page 143. List three countries in South America where the people do not speak Spanish or Portuguese.**

This square in Mexico City has been the center of Aztec, Spanish, and modern life.

Latin America Today

Europeans Arrive

Many Spanish colonists came to Latin America with Christopher Columbus in 1493, hoping to find gold. Others were farmers.

➤ **What were two main reasons Spanish colonists wanted to go to Latin America?**

Colonies Become Countries

During the 1500s, the French, Dutch, and English started colonies of their own in Latin America. But it was the Spanish who took over most of the land in Latin America. Explorers looking for gold spread out in every direction. Even if they did not find gold, they claimed the lands they found for Spain.

Spain ruled much of Latin America for about 300 years. But during that time, the colonies slowly changed. People whose families had come from Spain a hundred years earlier no longer thought of themselves as Spanish citizens. They wanted to govern their own land. But the king of Spain would not allow the Spanish colonists to form their own governments.

Then, in 1775, the colonies of North America began their war of independence against Great Britain. The people of Latin America watched this war very closely. When Great Britain lost the war, the colonies of Latin America were ready to fight for their own independence.

Haiti was the first country to win its independence, in 1804. Mexico began the fight for its independence in 1808. However, it was a long struggle. Mexico finally won its independence in 1821. But others did not become independent until the 1900s.

➤ **Look at the map on page 143. Name two countries that won their independence in the same year as Mexico.**

_____

One of the longest wars for independence was fought in the northern part of South America. There, colonists fought the Spanish for ten years. The colonists were led by Simón Bolívar, a rich landowner from Venezuela. In 1814, Bolívar took over the city of Bogotá, which is now the capital of Colombia. This was a great victory for Bolívar. To win Bogotá, Bolívar had to lead his army through the freezing Andes Mountains. The Spanish were not prepared when Bolívar's troops came out of the mountains.

144

The Spanish did not believe an army could cross the Andes. They were almost right! Before Bolívar even reached the mountains, he had to cross the plains during the rainy season. For a week, his soldiers walked through mud. At times they had to go through water that came up to their waists.

Travel was even harder for the soldiers once they began to climb the Andes. Their clothing was not warm enough, and some of them froze to death. But Bolívar's army was finally able to surprise the Spanish, and the colonists won the battle.

Independence

However, the war for independence did not end for another ten years. When the Spanish finally left South America in 1824, four new countries had formed: Colombia, Ecuador, Peru, and Venezuela. In 1825, part of Peru became a separate country. It was named Bolivia, after Bolívar.

➤ **Look at the map on page 143. Find Colombia, Ecuador, Peru, Venezuela, and Bolivia. Trace their borders.**

A Mexican vaquero

Independence did not make things better for many people in the new countries of Latin America. Now the rich landowners ran the government, but they did not know how to govern. They had never done it before. The landowners made laws that were good for them. But the laws did not help the other people in Latin America. Poor people in many countries were not much better off than they had been before independence. But the slaves that worked the plantations in Latin America finally won their freedom. Simón Bolívar helped pass a law that ended slavery in the lands he helped set free.

In the early 1900s, many people in Latin America worked hard to make their countries more modern. They improved their farms and grew more crops. They also built many factories and schools. Today, nations from Argentina to Mexico produce many goods that are sold all over the world.

Latin America's Largest City

A few years ago, workers were building a subway in Mexico City, the capital of Mexico. Suddenly, they hit stone. They had found a buried Aztec temple. The temple had once been part of an old Aztec city called Tenochtitlán. As archaeologists soon discovered, this city had many temples that were much bigger than the one the subway workers found.

In the 1500s, the Spanish destroyed most of Tenochtitlán. Then they built Mexico City on top of the ruins. Mexico City became the capital of the Spanish colony of New Spain. Mexico won its independence from Spain in 1821. Mexico City was now the capital of Mexico. The city's population grew throughout the 1800s and 1900s.

Mexico City is still growing. Every year thousands of Mexicans move to the capital. The population of Mexico City is above 18 million. Mexico City is not only the largest city in Latin America, it is the second-largest city in the world!

➤ **Find Mexico City on the map on page 143. Circle it on the map.**

Like all large cities, Mexico City has many different kinds of buildings. It has modern **skyscrapers**, tall buildings made out of steel and glass. It still has houses and churches built by the Spanish hundreds of years ago.

An avenue in Mexico City

Latin America Today

Mexico City also has many problems. One of the problems is **overcrowding**. This happens when there is not enough space for the people who want to live in an area. In Mexico City, there are not enough homes for all the people who move there. Some people live in run-down slum areas.

Why do so many Mexicans want to move to Mexico City? It is partly because there are more jobs in the city. Industrialization has created more jobs. **Industrialization** is the change a country makes when its economy moves from farming to making goods in factories. People who used to work on farms go to work in factories instead.

Latin American countries are building more factories. Industrialization often brings changes that are not welcome. In Mexico City, air pollution is a serious problem. Smoke from factories and fumes from cars and trucks have made the air dirty and hard to breathe.

Many Latin American countries have the same problems as Mexico. Some countries have destroyed valuable natural resources. For example, part of the Amazon rain forest in Brazil has been cut down for lumber and to clear land for farms.

The countries of Latin America must find a way to deal with the problems caused by industrialization and overpopulation. There are no easy answers. But some countries, such as Mexico and Costa Rica in Central America, have taken action. Mexico has passed laws to control air pollution caused by cars and trucks. Costa Rica has set up a tree-replanting program to save its forests.

➤ **Why is the air in Mexico City hard to breathe?**

_____

_____

Traffic in Mexico City

Cuba

Cuba is an island nation only 90 miles south of Florida. Havana is the capital of Cuba. The climate is very mild. People grow coffee, rice, corn, citrus fruits, and tobacco. But the most important crop on the island is sugar. The economy of the island depends mainly on growing sugar and making it usable.

In 1959, a communist dictator named Fidel Castro came to power on the island. After Castro took over, many Cubans fled the island nation and came to the United States. Over the years, more Cubans have left the island.

In 1961, the United States announced it would not trade with Cuba. It hoped that ending trade with Cuba would bring an end to communism. Even in 2006, the United States and Cuba were still not trade partners.

The Cuban government formed trade partnerships with the Soviet Union and China. Now, with the breakup of the Soviet Union, Cuba is more and more on its own. In 1995, Cuba announced that it would allow foreign businesses to operate in Cuba. Some people viewed the announcement as a sign that communism was losing strength in Cuba.

Many Cubans who left Cuba settled in Florida, where they have created a very successful community, especially in Miami. Many people in this Cuban-American community are against Castro and would like to see the end of communism in Cuba.

➤ **What communist dictator came to power in Cuba in 1959?**

Capitol Building in Havana, Cuba

Chapter Checkup ✓

➤ **Darken the circle by the answer that best completes each sentence.**

1. For more than 300 years, much of Latin America was ruled by
   (A) Great Britain.
   (B) Brazil.
   (C) Spain.
   (D) France.

2. Early colonists in Latin America came there to
   (A) climb the Andes.
   (B) farm and find gold.
   (C) look for slaves.
   (D) look for Mexico City.

3. Simón Bolívar helped many colonies in Latin America
   (A) give up farming.
   (B) become industrialized.
   (C) build factories and schools.
   (D) win independence from Spain.

4. The rich landowners were not good governors because
   (A) they were busy fighting wars.
   (B) they freed the slaves.
   (C) they wanted independence.
   (D) they had never governed before.

5. Many Latin American countries today are changing from farming to
   (A) making goods in factories.
   (B) independence.
   (C) pollution.
   (D) cities.

6. One of the problems in Latin America today is
   (A) the destruction of natural resources.
   (B) modern skyscrapers.
   (C) Spanish colonists.
   (D) difficult travel through the Andes.

Thinking & Writing

What problems do you think Simón Bolívar had fighting a war for ten years? Explain your answer.

_____

_____

_____

_____

_____

_____

_____

Name _____   Date _____

Unit 5 | **Skill Builder** | **Using an Elevation Map**

Remember that an elevation map shows how high above or below sea level the land is in a certain area. You can compare land regions with an elevation map.

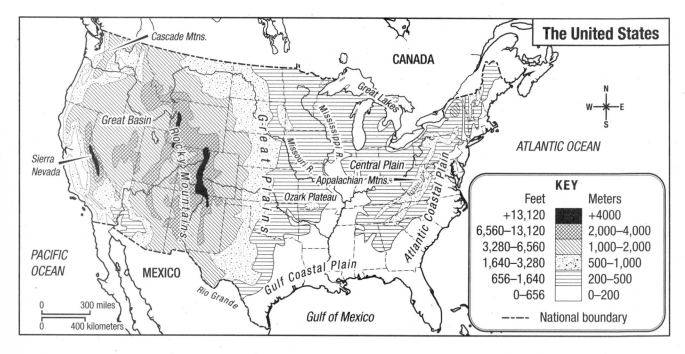

1. Which is lower, the Gulf Coastal Plain or the Great Plains?

_____

2. Besides the Sierra Nevada, what other mountains reach the highest elevations in the United States?

_____

3. What is the highest elevation of the Appalachian Mountains?

_____

4. Locate the area where you live on the map. What is the elevation in the area where you live?

_____

Unit 5  Test

➤ **Darken the circle by the answer that best completes each sentence.**

1. The Panama Canal is important because it shortens the distance between the Atlantic Ocean and
   (A) the Pacific Ocean.
   (B) the Caribbean Sea.
   (C) Panama.
   (D) the United States.

2. The Amazon River flows from the Andes Mountains to the
   (A) Pacific Ocean.
   (B) Gulf of Mexico.
   (C) Caribbean Sea.
   (D) Atlantic Ocean.

3. Canada's northern lands, the Yukon Territory, Northwest Territories, and Nunavut,
   (A) are good farmland.
   (B) are rich in oil and minerals.
   (C) have many French-speaking citizens.
   (D) are ruled by Great Britain.

4. The two main languages in Canada are English and
   (A) Italian.
   (B) Spanish.
   (C) French.
   (D) Russian.

5. The largest city in Latin America is
   (A) Mexico City.
   (B) Bogotá.
   (C) Rio de Janeiro.
   (D) Buenos Aires.

6. Industrialization in Latin America has created more jobs, and it has also
   (A) helped some countries win independence.
   (B) caused serious pollution problems.
   (C) helped some countries solve overcrowding problems.
   (D) caused many people to move out of Mexico City.

How have the geography and climate of North America contributed to the wealth of the United States and Canada?

_____

_____

_____

_____

_____

_____

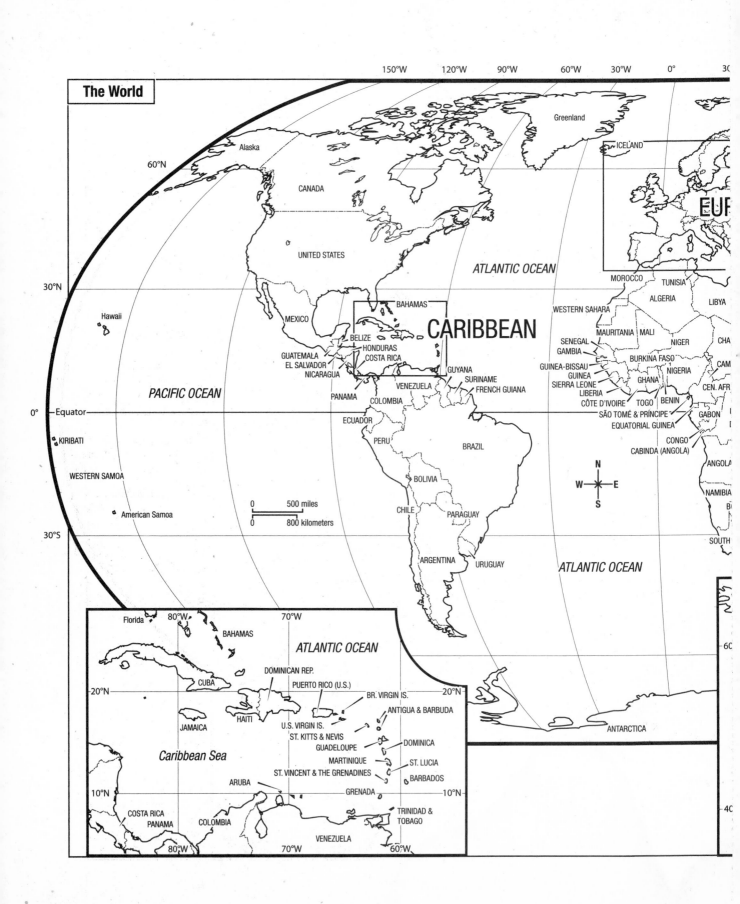

The World

Name _____   Date _____

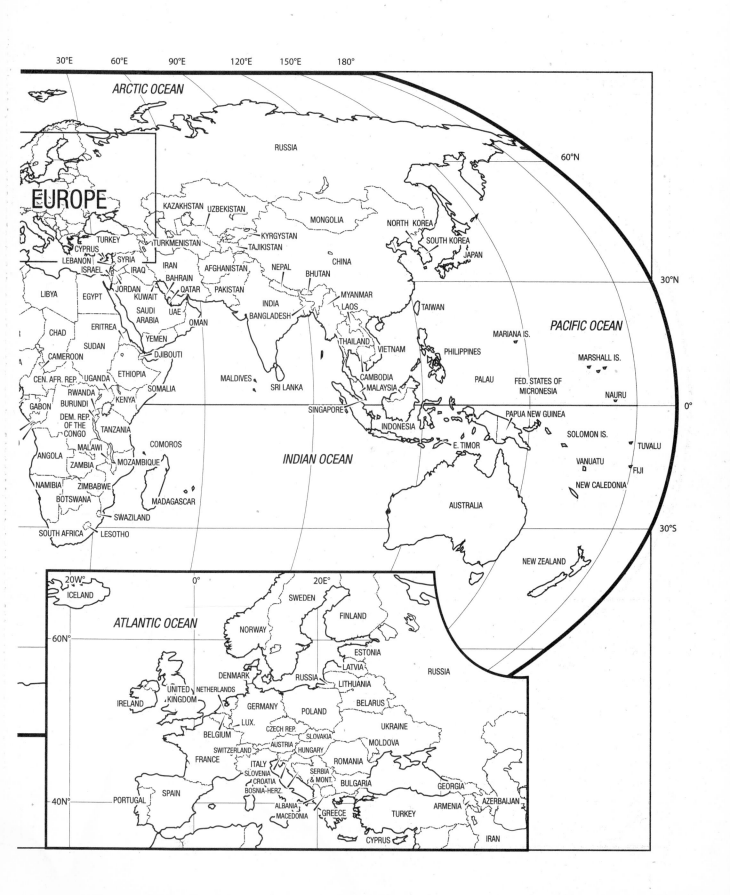

ARCTIC OCEAN

30°E 60°E 90°E 120°E 150°E 180°

60°N

RUSSIA

EUROPE

KAZAKHSTAN UZBEKISTAN
MONGOLIA
KYRGYSTAN
TURKEY
TURKMENISTAN TAJIKISTAN
CYPRUS
LEBANON SYRIA IRAN NEPAL CHINA
ISRAEL IRAQ AFGHANISTAN BHUTAN
JORDAN BAHRAIN
LIBYA EGYPT KUWAIT QATAR PAKISTAN MYANMAR
SAUDI UAE INDIA LAOS
ARABIA OMAN BANGLADESH
CHAD ERITREA YEMEN THAILAND VIETNAM
SUDAN
CAMEROON DJIBOUTI MALDIVES CAMBODIA
CEN. AFR. REP. ETHIOPIA SRI LANKA MALAYSIA
RWANDA SOMALIA SINGAPORE
GABON BURUNDI KENYA
DEM. REP. INDONESIA
OF THE
CONGO TANZANIA
MALAWI COMOROS
ANGOLA ZAMBIA MOZAMBIQUE
NAMIBIA ZIMBABWE
BOTSWANA MADAGASCAR
SWAZILAND
SOUTH AFRICA LESOTHO

NORTH KOREA
SOUTH KOREA JAPAN

30°N

TAIWAN

PACIFIC OCEAN

MARIANA IS.

PHILIPPINES MARSHALL IS.

PALAU FED. STATES OF
MICRONESIA NAURU

PAPUA NEW GUINEA 0°

SOLOMON IS. TUVALU

E. TIMOR VANUATU
FIJI
NEW CALEDONIA

INDIAN OCEAN

AUSTRALIA

30°S

NEW ZEALAND

20W° 0° 20E°
ICELAND SWEDEN
ATLANTIC OCEAN FINLAND
NORWAY 60N°
ESTONIA
LATVIA RUSSIA
DENMARK RUSSIA LITHUANIA
UNITED NETHERLANDS BELARUS
IRELAND KINGDOM GERMANY
LUX. POLAND UKRAINE
BELGIUM CZECH REP. SLOVAKIA
SWITZERLAND AUSTRIA MOLDOVA
FRANCE HUNGARY
ITALY ROMANIA
SLOVENIA SERBIA
CROATIA & MONT. BULGARIA GEORGIA
BOSNIA-HERZ. 40N°
PORTUGAL SPAIN ALBANIA ARMENIA AZERBAIJAN
MACEDONIA GREECE TURKEY
CYPRUS IRAN

WORLD MAP
Core Skills Social Studies 6, SV 9781419039058

Glossary

aborigine (page 122) An aborigine is one of the first people to live in a place. The early people of Australia are known today as the Aborigines.

agora (page 57) The agora was a big open area in ancient Athens where people bought and sold things.

alms (page 104) Alms are money or gifts to help the poor. Giving alms is one of the Five Pillars of Islam.

Amazon Basin (page 133) The Amazon Basin is a large, flat, bowl-like area of land covered by a rain forest in South America. The Amazon River runs through it.

archaeologists (page 5) Archaeologists study artifacts and other things to learn how humans lived long ago.

archipelago (page 115) An archipelago is a group of islands.

artifacts (page 5) Artifacts are objects made and left by people who lived long ago.

bloc (page 89) A bloc is a part of something. After World War II, Europe was divided into a Soviet bloc and a Western bloc.

boomerang (page 123) A boomerang is a curved, flat piece of wood or animal bone. Boomerangs were used by the Aborigines of Australia to hunt animals.

boycott (page 100) A boycott is when people agree not to buy from or sell to a person, business, or nation. A boycott is used to make change happen.

Canadian Shield (page 130) The Canadian Shield is the large, mainly flat region around Hudson Bay in Canada.

canal (page 132) A canal is a path dug by people so that water can cross land.

caravan (page 50) A caravan is a group of people and animals that travel together.

caste (page 41) A caste is a group that does the same type of work. The Aryans in India divided people into castes. People were born into castes.

cathedral (page 70) A cathedral is a large and important church.

Christianity (page 64) Christianity is a religion based on the teachings of Jesus.

citizen (page 56) A citizen is a person who is a member of a country.

civil disobedience (page 109) Civil disobedience is when people break the law because they believe the law is wrong or unfair. People do this to protest these kinds of laws.

civilization (page 27) Civilization is the way of life of a group of people or a nation. Civilization includes the art, science, economy, and government of a people.

clan (page 116) A clan is a group of families that belongs to a larger family group.

climate (page 14) Climate is the kind of weather a place has over time.

cold war (page 90) A cold war is a war fought with words and ideas instead of weapons. The Cold War was a time of little trust between the United States and the former Soviet Union after World War II.

colony (page 55) A colony is land and people ruled by another country or parent state.

comedy (page 58) A comedy is a play with a funny, happy ending.

common law (page 76) Common law was a group of laws set up in England by Henry II. These laws applied to everyone.

commune (page 114) A commune is a group of people working together. In China, a commune is a group of farms where the land is joined together in a single unit.

communicate (page 8) To communicate means to share ideas and information.

communism (page 88) Communism is a kind of government in which most or all land and businesses are owned by the government. Under communism, people cannot choose their leaders.

community (page 4) A community is a group of people living and working together.

conquer (page 30) To conquer means to defeat or to win. The Babylonians conquered the Sumerians.

conservation (page 21) Conservation is saving Earth's resources, such as water, forests, air, and soil.

convict (page 124) A convict is a person who is serving a sentence for breaking the law.

Crusades (page 70) The Crusades were the journeys made by the Christians to fight the Muslims. The Christians fought the Muslims to capture Jerusalem.

culture (page 6) Culture is a way of living shared by a group of people.

cuneiform (page 29) Cuneiform is a form of writing that was used in Mesopotamia.

current (page 83) A current is a warm or cool stream of water. The Gulf Stream is a current that flows on the surface of the ocean.

democracy (page 57) Democracy is a kind of government. There is no king. The people have power in this type of government.

desert (page 15) A desert is an area that gets very little rain.

dictator (page 63) A dictator is a ruler who has all the power in a country.

diplomat (page 88) A diplomat is a person who helps his or her nation work with other nations.

distance scale (page 40) A distance scale is used to compare a distance on a map to a distance on Earth.

domesticate (page 28) To domesticate means to tame wild animals so that they can be used by people.

drought (page 31) A drought is a long period of time without rain.

dynasty (page 43) A dynasty is a family who rules over a land. A dynasty takes place over many years and generations.

economy (page 6) An economy is the way people make, buy, and sell things.

elevation map (page 136) An elevation map shows the actual height of mountains, plateaus, plains, and other landforms in feet or meters.

emperor (page 64) An emperor is a person who rules an empire.

empire (page 60) An empire is a large area of land that is ruled by one person or a small group.

erosion (page 16) Erosion is the wearing away of land by wind, water, or glacial ice.

Exodus (page 31) The Exodus occurred when Moses led the Hebrews out of Egypt. Exodus means "departure."

extended family (page 105) An extended family includes parents, children, grandparents, aunts, uncles, and cousins.

faith (page 104) Faith is the belief in a god or gods. Faith is one of the Five Pillars of Islam.

fasting (page 104) Fasting means to go without eating. Fasting is one of the Five Pillars of Islam.

fertile (page 28) Fertile land is good for growing crops.

feudalism (page 68) Feudalism was a system of government during the Middle Ages. Powerful people agreed to protect those less powerful. In return, the less powerful people fought or worked for the powerful people.

fjord (page 131) A fjord is a long, narrow bay that lies between high mountains.

fuel (page 19) Fuel is anything that can be burned to give power and heat.

geography (page 11) Geography is the study of Earth and how we live on it.

glacier (page 15) A glacier is a huge field of ice.

glasnost (page 92) Glasnost was a plan for openness in the former Soviet Union. Mikhail Gorbachev promised the people more freedom with glasnost.

government (page 6) A government is a group of people who make the laws and lead others.

grid (page 82) A grid is the pattern of parallels and meridians that cross each other like the lines in a net. Grids are used on maps to find places.

guild (page 71) A guild was a group of people with the same job during the Middle Ages.

hemisphere (page 81) A hemisphere is one half of the globe or Earth.

hieroglyphics (page 37) Hieroglyphics, or picture writing, was the writing system used by the ancient Egyptians.

highland (page 11) A highland is hilly land between flat land and mountains.

Hinduism (page 42) Hinduism is a religion followed by many people in India.

imperialism (page 98) Imperialism is when one country controls the economy and government of another country.

independence (page 95) Independence is freedom from the control of others.

Industrial Revolution (page 77) The Industrial Revolution was a time when new machines and industries made a great change in how people lived.

industrialization (page 147) Industrialization is the change a country makes when its economy changes from farming to making goods in factories.

irrigate (page 30) To irrigate means to bring water to dry land, usually by ditches and canals, so that crops will grow.

Islam (page 103) Islam is the religion followed by Muslims. It was founded by Muhammad, who was told there was only one god, named Allah.

Judaism (page 31) Judaism is the religion of the Jews.

knight (page 68) A knight was a man who fought for his king or for other nobles during the Middle Ages.

legal (page 65) Legal means lawful.

lines of latitude (page 82) Lines of latitude are imaginary lines that run east to west around Earth. Lines of latitude are also called parallels.

lines of longitude (page 82) Lines of longitude are imaginary lines that run north to south around Earth. Lines of longitude are also called meridians.

lock (page 132) A lock is a gated area in a canal where a ship can be raised from one level to another. Locks look like a set of steps.

Magna Carta (page 76) The Magna Carta was a charter signed in 1215 by King John of England. It limited the power of the English king.

manor (page 68) A manor was a small community where most people lived in the Middle Ages. A manor included a noble's house, a small village, a church, a mill, and fields and woods.

Maori (page 123) The Maori were the first people to live in New Zealand. They still live there today.

monk (page 69) A monk is a man who gives up everything to lead a religious life.

monotheism (page 31) Monotheism is the belief in one god.

monsoon (page 85) A monsoon is a wind that blows in one direction in the summer, bringing heavy rains. A monsoon blows in a different direction in the winter, bringing dry air.

mountain (page 11) A mountain is an area of land that rises far above sea level.

multiculturalism (page 139) Multiculturalism is a program that teaches people about different cultures.

mummification (page 35) Mummification was the way the Egyptians protected a dead body. They put chemicals on the body and wrapped it in cloth. Finally, they covered the wrapped body in a mixture like tar.

Muslim (page 70) A Muslim is a person who follows the religion of Islam.

nation (page 75) A nation is a large group of people who share the same country and government, and often the same language and history.

natural environment (page 5) The natural environment is the air, water, land, plants, and animals around us.

noble (page 68) A noble was a rich and powerful person during the Middle Ages. A noble was less powerful than a king.

nomad (page 102) A nomad is a person who moves from place to place looking for food and water.

nonrenewable resource (page 20) A nonrenewable resource is something from nature that cannot be made again. Coal and oil are examples of nonrenewable resources.

nonviolent (page 109) A nonviolent person is someone who does not physically fight to get something done. A nonviolent person uses peaceful ways to get something done.

nun (page 69) A nun is a woman who gives up everything to lead a religious life.

oasis (page 86) An oasis is a place in the desert where there is water. The water is from an underground spring in the desert.

opium (page 112) Opium is a dangerous drug.

outback (page 122) The outback is a large area of hot, dry plains in Australia.

overcrowding (page 147) Overcrowding happens when there is not enough space for people to live in an area.

papyrus (page 37) Papyrus is a kind of paper made by the ancient Egyptians from plants growing along the Nile.

patrician (page 62) A patrician was a rich person in ancient Rome.

Pax Romana (page 64) The Pax Romana ("Roman peace") was the time during the ancient Roman Empire when there was no fighting. It lasted about 200 years. The Pax Romana began with the rule of Augustus.

peninsula (page 83) A peninsula is land with water on three sides.

petroleum (page 105) Petroleum is oil. Gas for cars is made from petroleum.

pharaoh (page 34) A pharaoh was a king or queen of ancient Egypt.

pilgrimage (page 104) A pilgrimage is a trip made for religious reasons. Making a pilgrimage to Mecca is one of the Five Pillars of Islam.

plain (page 11) A plain is a low, flat area of land.

plantation (page 96) A plantation is a very large farm.

plateau (page 11) A plateau is a high, flat area of land.

plebeian (page 62) A plebeian was a common person in ancient Rome.

pollution (page 22) Pollution is the dirtying of the air, water, or soil.

pope (page 70) The pope is the leader of the Roman Catholic Church.

poverty (page 113) Poverty is the condition of being poor.

prayer (page 104) Prayer is the act of praying to a god or gods. Prayer is important in many religions.

precipitation (page 17) Precipitation is moisture, such as rain, snow, and hail.

prime meridian (page 81) The prime meridian is an imaginary line that divides Earth into the Eastern and Western Hemispheres.

Protestant (page 74) A Protestant is a member of any of several Christian churches that split off from the Roman Catholic Church.

pyramid (page 36) A pyramid is a stone building with four sides that are shaped like triangles. The Egyptians used pyramids as tombs.

racism (page 97) Racism is the belief that people of some races are better than people of other races.

rain forest (page 14) A rain forest is a very thick forest in an area where rainfall is very heavy all year long.

rebel (page 113) A rebel is a person who is not happy with the way things are and wants to change them.

reform (page 113) A reform is a change to try to make things better.

renewable resource (page 19) A renewable resource is something from nature that can be made again. Trees and fish are renewable resources.

republic (page 62) A republic is a form of government where people choose their leaders.

resource (page 19) A resource is something used by people to meet their needs.

savanna (page 47) A savanna is a grassy plain with few or no trees.

secede (page 140) To secede is to leave a nation and become a separate nation. Many people who live in Quebec would like Quebec to secede from Canada.

serf (page 68) A serf was a common person who farmed the land during the Middle Ages.

skyscraper (page 146) A skyscraper is a tall building made of steel and glass.

slave (page 31) A slave is a person who is owned by another person.

strike (page 91) A strike is when people stop working until they get what they want.

technology (page 7) Technology means the tools, materials, and knowledge people use to make things.

temple (page 30) A temple is a building where people pray to a god or gods.

textiles (page 76) Textiles are cloth.

tomb (page 35) A tomb is a place or building where the dead are buried.

tragedy (page 58) A tragedy is a play with a sad ending.

tundra (page 84) A tundra is a cold, treeless area where the land is always frozen. Much of Alaska, Canada, and Russia is tundra.

union (page 91) A union is a group of workers who work together for a special reason. Often, unions try to get better working conditions and better pay for their workers.

vassal (page 68) A vassal was a noble given land by the king or another noble during the Middle Ages. In return for the land, the vassal promised to fight the king's or other noble's enemies.

ziggurat (page 30) A ziggurat was the temple at the center of a Sumerian city.

Answer Key

NOTE: For answers not provided, check that students have given an appropriate response and/or followed the directions given.

Page 8

Slowest: by jet; Fastest: by wagon train

Page 9

9 A.M.

Page 10

1. C   **2.** A   **3.** B   **4.** C   **5.** A   **6.** D

Answers will vary. Accept all reasonable answers.

Page 11

mountains

Page 12

plains, mountains

Page 14

tropical, dry, moist warm, moist cold, arctic, highland

Page 15

above the Tropic of Cancer

Page 16

arctic regions

Page 17

People do not usually live in regions that do not receive much rain.

Page 18

1. C   **2.** B   **3.** A   **4.** A   **5.** D   **6.** C

Answers will vary. Accept all reasonable answers.

Page 20

Students should name any two of the following: North America, Asia, Europe, and Australia.

Page 24

1. B   **2.** A   **3.** C   **4.** B   **5.** A   **6.** D

Answers will vary. Accept all reasonable answers.

Page 25

1. 8:00 P.M.

2. two

3. 7:30 A.M.

4. You would set it back one hour.

Page 26

1. B   **2.** C   **3.** A   **4.** B   **5.** C   **6.** B

Answers will vary. Accept all reasonable answers.

Page 28

Nineveh, Babylon, Lagash, Ur

Page 30

northwest

Page 31

drought

Page 32

1. C   **2.** B   **3.** D   **4.** A   **5.** A   **6.** D

Answers will vary. Accept all reasonable answers.

Page 39

1. C   **2.** A   **3.** D   **4.** A   **5.** C   **6.** B

Answers will vary. Accept all reasonable answers.

Page 40

about 1,300 miles

Page 42

Both believed in life after death.

Page 45

1. D   **2.** C   **3.** D   **4.** A   **5.** D   **6.** D

Answers will vary. Accept all reasonable answers.

Page 51

1. C   **2.** B   **3.** B   **4.** D   **5.** D   **6.** B

Answers will vary. Accept all reasonable answers.

Page 52

1. about 400 miles

2. inset map; about 110 kilometers

3. about 120 miles on both maps

Page 53

1. B   **2.** A   **3.** C   **4.** B   **5.** A   **6.** C

Answers will vary. Accept all reasonable answers.

Page 54

Ionian Sea, Mediterranean Sea, Aegean Sea

Page 58

every four years

Page 59

1. B   **2.** A   **3.** B   **4.** D   **5.** A   **6.** C

Answers will vary. Accept all reasonable answers.

Page 60

about 550 miles

Page 61

London: northwest; Carthage: southwest; Danube River: north, northeast; Egypt: southeast

Page 62

about 300 miles

Page 64

They believed in only one god.

Page 65

First Olympic Games were held 776 years before Jesus was born; 464 years passed between first Olympic Games and work on the first Roman road; three centuries passed between birth of Jesus and end of persecution of Christians; 1,000 years passed between formation of Greek city-states and beginning of persecution of Christians.

Page 66

1. D   2. B   3. D   4. C   5. A   6. C

Answers will vary. Accept all reasonable answers.

Page 68

Both had knights.

Page 72

1. A   2. C   3. A   4. B   5. D   6. A

Answers will vary. Accept all reasonable answers.

Page 73

Athens

Page 75

Papal States

Page 78

1. D   2. C   3. A   4. C   5. A   6. B

Answers will vary. Accept all reasonable answers.

Page 79

1. fall of Roman Empire
2. 800
3. Students should mark 1187 on the time line and add the label *Muslims recapture Jerusalem.*
4. 717
5. Students should bracket the time span from 476 to 1500 in some way and indicate with a label that those years are the Middle Ages.

Page 80

1. D   2. A   3. C   4. B   5. A   6. C

Answers will vary. Accept all reasonable answers.

Page 81

Western Hemisphere

Page 82

Memphis; prime meridian or 0°

Page 87

1. B   2. A   3. D   4. B   5. D   6. C

Answers will vary. Accept all reasonable answers.

Page 89

Western bloc

Page 90

to keep people from escaping to West Berlin from East Berlin

Page 91

They wanted higher pay and free elections in Poland.

Page 94

1. A   2. C   3. C   4. B   5. D   6. C

Answers will vary. Accept all reasonable answers.

Page 98

France, Great Britain, Portugal, Belgium, Spain

Page 99

Chad, Central African Republic, Congo, Gabon, Cabinda

Page 100

boycotts

Page 101

1. B   2. B   3. A   4. C   5. C   6. D

Answers will vary. Accept all reasonable answers.

Page 102

about 300 miles

Page 103

Saudi Arabia; Red Sea

Page 106

9.3 million barrels per day; Oil production in the United States has been decreasing.

Page 107

1. D   2. B   3. A   4. C   5. C   6. B

Answers will vary. Accept all reasonable answers.

Page 112

about 900 miles

Page 113

1912; 1949

Page 115

4 islands; 140°E

Page 116

Sea of Japan

Page 118

35%; increase

Page 120

1. B   2. C   3. A   4. B   5. C   6. D

Answers will vary. Accept all reasonable answers.

Page 122

Canberra; Wellington; noon

Page 124

Tasmania; Tasman Sea

Page 125

1907

Page 126

1. C   2. D   3. B   4. A   5. D   6. A

Answers will vary. Accept all reasonable answers.

Page 127

1. no
2. about 890 million
3. about 1985
4. Students will probably say yes. The graph shows that India had a population of about 1 billion in 2000. If it grows at the same rate, it could reach 1.5 billion by 2010.

Page 128

1. B   2. A   3. D   4. C   5. B   6. A

Answers will vary. Accept all reasonable answers.

Page 129

Atlantic Ocean

Page 130

warmer

Page 131

mountains and plains

Page 132

around the southern tip of South America

Page 135

1. B   2. D   3. A   4. C   5. D   6. A

Answers will vary. Accept all reasonable answers.

Page 136

2,000 to 4,000 feet

Page 141

1. A   2. D   3. C   4. B   5. B   6. D

Answers will vary. Accept all reasonable answers.

Page 142

Guyana, Suriname, French Guiana

Page 144

Costa Rica, El Salvador, Venezuela

Page 148

Fidel Castro

Page 149

1. C   2. B   3. D   4. D   5. A   6. A

Answers will vary. Accept all reasonable answers.

Page 150

1. the Gulf Coastal Plain
2. the Rocky Mountains
3. 3,280–6,560 feet
4. Answers will vary. Accept all reasonable answers.

Page 151

1. A   2. D   3. B   4. C   5. A   6. B

Answers will vary. Accept all reasonable answers.